HOW TO BE A SUCCESSFUL FREELANCE TRANSLATOR:

Make Translation Work for You

Robert Gebhardt

D1538568

LUGANO
TRANSLATIONS

Table of Contents

Introduction to the Third Edition

A lot has changed since I first wrote this book. I remember sitting in Notch Coffee shop in Taipei writing the first edition. At that point I was dating a girl, taking Chinese lessons, and traveling around Taiwan and China as much as I could.

And now, 5 years later, I have married that girl and we have a daughter together. We are living in Charlotte, USA and are (slightly) more settled. We have been living around Asia (Taipei, Taiwan and Shanghai, China), Europe (Lugano, Switzerland and Lucca, Italy) and the United States (Atlanta, DC and now, Charlotte) while growing my business.

And my work has been changing as well. I've been expanding from freelance translation into setting up a boutique (i.e. small) translation agency. But I am obviously still translating, and I've also been coaching and helping out other budding freelance translators.

The translation industry itself has been changing too. I remember people talking about how Google Translate and other online tools would make our profession obsolete. And yet the global market for outsourced language services continues to grow, hitting $46 billion in 2018, and on track to reach $56 billion by 2021[1].

I've updated this to incorporate all the changes that have been occurring. This new edition includes new information that has come up thanks to input from other translators, as well as other readers, students in my class, and followers of my YouTube channel.

Of course, changes have been occurring (and are still occurring) for all participants. From translators, to agencies to end clients. While many of these changes may make us uncomfortable, they should never be ignored. This edition will address the market as it stands now, including the recent changes in terms of technology, legalities and current trends. Things will continue changing, but I try to lay out the information so as to make it as permanent as possible.

At the end of the book, I will also include a short section on setting up your own agency, in case

---

[1] If you are curious as to why this is happening, I wrote an article addressing this here: https://medium.com/@oceanlugano/is-freelance-translation-worth-it-951142074373

this is something you are interested in. I am still in the process of growing my own agency, but in the meantime, I've come across a great deal of information, both good and bad. So I thought it would be worth sharing what I've seen and been through. I will also include some links in case you are interested in some of my services, such as Resume/Profile page reviews, 1-on-1 consulting, etc.

How to Be a Successful Freelance Translator

How would you like to be able to set your own hours, pick your own clients, decide where you want to work, and what you want to wear while you work? How would you like to work from a coffee shop, from the beach, or from Thailand? Does it sound too good to be true? Well, it is.

Plenty of people are doing exactly that. In fact, I am one of them. I currently live in Charlotte, USA. My clients are in the United States, Europe, and China, and I work with translators on four different continents. I've also been living around Asia (Taiwan, Shanghai, Seoul), Europe (Lugano, Switzerland and Lucca, Italy) and the United States (Atlanta, DC and now, Charlotte) while growing my business. In the meantime, I've taken lessons in Chinese, traveled all over the place, done a little modeling, and am writing this book. Oh, I also am married with a 1 year-old daughter.

So why is it too good to be true? Because, as with anything in life, it isn't that simple. As with anything in life, it takes hard work, dedication, motivation, persistence, and possibly more of that boring stuff you always hear about before you tune out.

But don't get discouraged just yet; at least finish this chapter before getting discouraged! The good news is this book contains step-by-step instructions on how to make it possible. Obviously, everyone's experience is different, and it is possible that you are already following a few of the points I mention. But following these steps is a great outline of how I achieved this life, and how you can too.

I should just repeat this one more time. **It is not easy.** I worked my tail off, and I am still working my tail off. I doubt I have more free time than your average worker, but I do get to choose which clients to work with and when to work with them.

This is not a *"here are the secrets all the industry experts don't want you to know"* type book (For the record, those are all scams). Also, your specific path may vary from what is written here. But, like any instruction manual, it's good to have read it, even if later you decide to do things a bit differently.

In this book, I will show you how to create a strong web presence, how to highlight your strengths, and how to get it in front of potential clients. Then, I will show various methods of getting paid by clients (and how to make sure they actually pay you), as well as how to rinse and repeat, so you can do this for a living. At the end of the book, I also describe how to take your translation skills to the next level, how to have translators work for you so you get to sit back and relax and let someone else do the work for a change if you want to.

I should also mention that I have very few, if any, translation tips. I'm pretty much assuming you are all translators and you're good at what you do. If you weren't then you wouldn't be seeking a career in this field. If you would like more general translation tips, I recommend checking out the forums on ProZ.com and wordreference.com where you can also post your own queries.

Lastly, I will mention many products and brand names here. Some favorably, some less so. I promise that **none** of them are paying me anything. I am subscribed to a couple for my own purposes, but I have no incentive to talk one up and talk another one down. My only incentive is giving you the best information I can, based on my experience.

"Wait wait wait! But I don't have a degree in translation. In fact, I never studied it in school. Can I still be a translator?"

Well, the truth is I have no degree in translation, whether from University, Graduate school, or anywhere else. In fact, I may as well address this first question that you may have right away: **you do not need to have a degree in translation in order to be a translator**. If anyone tells you that you do, point them in my direction. I earn a living from translation with degrees in business and finance/economics.

Having a degree seems to vary from place to place. In Europe it is much more common for translators to have a degree in translation, while in the United States it is more common to have a degree in your area of specialization. In my experience whether you have one or the other doesn't make too much difference to clients. The important thing is to use the knowledge you have, which is what this book will help you do.

So, are you ready to work for yourself, to decide which clients you want to deal with and when? Are you ready to decide where you want to work and how much time you want to spend working? And are you ready to earn these benefits through your sweat equity?

Great! Let's get started.

Well, actually, not just yet. Let's start with what to do even before getting started.

Read on...

•Before Getting Started

•Let's Take a Step Back with Some Theory

•Starting Strategy

•Finding Clients

•Marketing

•Good Problems: You've Won an Assignment. Now What?

•Getting Paid

•Other Tips and Tricks to Keep in Mind

•Next Steps

WHERE WE DISCUSS ALL THE PREPARATION YOU WILL NEED TO START WORKING IN FREELANCE TRANSLATION

Before Getting Started

I know you're ready and itching to get started, and that's the exact motivation you need at this point. That's why these steps might seem either like a waste, or things you can get back to later. But trust me, you will need these. And why bother doing anything if you aren't going to do it well?

Anyway, since I know you want to get started, I've listed the time and/or money you will be spending for these first couple of tasks, just to give you an idea. As with any long journey, the key to the journey itself starts with preparation.

Pregame

(1 day maximum, or ½ day maximum if you already have a resume)

You should prepare a couple things before getting started:

1. an updated resume
2. a list of your services and specializations
3. a good photo of yourself (not glamour or professional, but one where you look like an approachable, friendly human being)
4. a personal website (or profile page)

Let's tackle these points one by one:

Updated Resume

This is actually not the most important point, but it helps to have a resume detailing any translation and writing associated material you may have. This can range from your personal blog (if it is still being kept up) to published articles, and anything in between.

If you don't have any published material or any real web presence, that's fine. Just detail your usual school and work history. **Being able to tie the anonymous online person to a real-life person goes a long way for the people hiring you.** When

18

you're online, people don't know who you are. They're handing you a job which they will then need to hand to their client. And it's likely that their professional reputation is tied to this job, so trust is key. As a freelancer rather than an in-house employee, gaps in your professional experience are not as important to them if they feel they can trust you.

These are some points to emphasize in your resume:

- languages *(obviously)*
- computer skills *(all your work will be on the computer, so this is important)*
- self-driven/entrepreneurial points *(showing that you're a self-starter)*
- specialization skills *(we'll discuss specializations in more detail later on, but for now these are the industries you will concentrate on. So, if you're going to carry out financial translations, then you should detail all the financial experience you have)*

It is also a good idea to have your resume in both your source and target languages, since you will likely have clients who do business in either one. If one of these languages (most likely your source language) is not your native tongue, then **don't be shy about hiring someone to proofread it** to make sure it is written correctly.

Also, keep in mind that different countries have different conventions for resume writing. So look up a few examples in each language first. For example, European Union countries may ask you for a photo, while United States companies are prohibited from doing so by law.

Remember that as a general rule, **nobody wants to read a resume**. Nobody enjoys reading the line-by-line bullet points with your carefully crafted words. So just get to the point and sell your skills and experience that are relevant to translation. Also - and this should go without saying – you are applying as a translator, or a language professional, so make sure your resume is well written and typo free!

Which Language Should You translate Into?

*As a general rule, a translator translates into their native tongue. If you are truly fluent in both the source and target languages, then either way is fine, but chances are, you feel more comfortable in one language than you do in the other. **The more comfortable language is your target language, while the other is your source language.** Interestingly, the opposite is true for interpreting. Here, the source language should be your native tongue so you can catch all the nuances in the speech.*

A couple of other points

- Remember to keep the same spelling for your name throughout your resume *(this goes for your list of services and Profile page as well).*
- Specifying your time zone can be helpful as well.
- Gaps in employment aren't all that important for freelancers, so don't worry about these too much. It is better to have a few gaps than to detail activities that have nothing to do with translation or with your specialization.
- Include any computer skills. As mentioned above, especially if you have desktop publishing (DTP) experience (this is always in high demand)!

Listing Your Specializations

This is separate from your resume, and it is also more important. This is the first thing a potential client will be looking through. They want to make sure you can offer the services they require. Their boss just told them their furniture warehouse website needs to be translated into Portuguese, and they don't know what to look for. Therefore, you'll need to show them you're the right person.

So, what is the correct strategy? Do you want to list as many specialties as possible? Or do you want to narrow it down to a minimal list? You can play around with this, but to start out, I recommend you be **very narrow in a macro sense and wide-ranging at a micro-level**.

In other words, for the **general services such as languages, narrow it down**. If you specialize in Portuguese, you can list that you are comfortable with the Brazil and Portugal variants, but then I would stop there. Don't list French, Spanish, Italian, Galician, and Basque, even if you know them. And most certainly don't list the Slavic and Germanic languages you know. To the potential

22

client, no one can know that many languages perfectly, so they'll assume you're exaggerating. And if you're exaggerating about your languages, who knows what else you're exaggerating about?

For specializations, however, you can be much more prolific. Your specializations are the industries that you feel comfortable translating in. So, if you studied and/or worked in the finance field and have experience translating income statements, then you probably feel much more comfortable translating financial documents than translating poetry. Having said this, it is a lot more acceptable to have various specializations than various languages. I find the best way to do this is to list several main specializations, with several other points, like this:

Main specializations:

> ➤ Business, economics, finance
> ➤ Legal, government, public affairs

Others:

> ➤ Video games, computers/IT
> ➤ History, religion
> ➤ Travel, miscellaneous

Of course, if you are not comfortable with any of these topics, do not list them. You will **not** be able to fake it. Just list whichever one of these you feel comfortable listing. Also include a miscellaneous section at the end. This doesn't mean anything precise, but it makes your specializations more open-ended.

Here is an example of my bio on ProZ.com (a translation website – we'll get to that). As you can see, I only have two languages listed, but I am quite liberal with my specializations, and even more so with my *"Also Works In"* section.

The tagline, which is right below my name, also clearly states *"Bilingual Italian-English"*. Your tagline will most likely catch everyone's eye at first, so make it clear and concise.

Keep in mind, however, that this becomes less and less important the more rare your language pair is. In fact, if your language pair is rare enough (say, Navajo-Spanish), then specializations might not be necessary to specify at all, and will probably add little or nothing to what you can offer.

Feel free to scour ProZ.com and Translatorscafe.com (you can read more about these in the chapter "*Setting Up Your Account*"), to take a look at other profiles and get ideas for how to structure your own. What catches your eye? What doesn't look good? If you aren't familiar with the layout, just remember that many recruiters are in the same boat as well. *(Personally I find their layout extremely complicated and I've been using their websites for close to ten years now!)*

Lying In Your Bio

A bio restates your resume, and obviously you should never lie in either one. Some people recommend twisting words, exaggerating, or being vague, but I don't. First of all, they are lies, and you know they are. Second, they're just bad business. Everyone, especially people paid to sift through resumes, can spot them. Third, if they're good enough not to be spotted, you risk having to complete a job you have no idea how to do. And finally, lying on your resume inevitably causes a downward spiral that leads to a life of crime and meth, both of which are bad for translators. So, don't waste time with odd wording. If you can translate one language to another, you have all that is needed. The rest is just fodder.

Your Photo

This is more important than you'd think. Right at the beginning, you're selling trust just as much, if not more, than your skills. Even if the potential client is outwardly searching for a good translator, their first impression will be quick and decisive, and your photo will have a lot to do with it. So, don't bother taking a glamour shot or a professional photo and avoid anything resembling a mug shot. Make it slightly candid, and don't worry about the quality (it won't be any bigger than 300 x 300 pixels on any of the provider websites).

In other words, this shouldn't be a reason to delay. If you're at a coffee shop right now, turn on your webcam and take a picture of yourself working at your computer with a cup of coffee in front of you. This is the image clients like to have of their freelancers. Alternatively, sift through your old photos and try to find one where you look like somebody you might want to have a beer or coffee with. Simply put, anywhere in between stiff as a board and drunk as a skunk.

I've also been told that smiling, or at least looking at the camera, conveys more trust. I have two profile photos I tend to use, one of them looking at the camera and the other one looking away. I can't say I have noticed too much difference. Then again, as you can see, the one looking at the camera isn't as serious. Which one do you prefer?

Here are the two pictures I am using. I use the one on the left more frequently, since it shows me in more of a working environment. I only use the one on the right when I feel a bit surer of myself (you can probably see why).

Your Website

This is absolutely essential and often overlooked. Your personal website is another touchpoint that ensures trust with the client. It shows commitment to what you do. I used to love the website https://about.me for this, since it offered exactly what was needed. Unfortunately, recently they have severely limited what can be done for free, and I'm not sure the paid version is worth it.

These days I generally recommend using your online Profile (ProZ.com and the like) or else your LinkedIn page. While these do not give you your own website per se, they do provide all the relevant information in one place in a professional design, plus they have built in SEO, which will make you easier to find on the web.

You can, of course, also purchase a domain and then create a free one page website through most registries, like godaddy.com. Alternatively you can have that domain redirect to the online profile page of your choice (most registries make it very easy to do this).

There are many reasons for using a ready-made website, rather than creating your own. First of all, it is cheaper and (much) less time-consuming. The main reason, however, is that the established websites, such as ProZ.com and LinkedIn, have built in SEO, which will inevitably be better than the SEO you'll be able to muster for your own personal website.

Search Engine Optimization (SEO)

When creating a website, a term that gets tossed around is Search Engine Optimization (SE0). You will hear that having your own website means you'll have to use certain keywords, tags, formats, and possibly buy Facebook ads or use Google AdWords. My advice here is not to worry about that. I have two reasons for this. First of all, you're not that good at it. If you aren't a techie person (and if you're just creating your website now, you probably aren't), then you won't be nearly as good as some other companies out there, no matter how hard you try. Second, even if you get very good, you still won't be as good as ProZ, Facebook, Twitter, or about.me. So why not just use these websites (including their SEO) and keep your profile prominent on them?

Remember, when making your personal page, resume, and personal photo, the task is not to show how cool, awesome, or intelligent you are. You just want to show:

1. Your trustworthiness
2. That you can totally, completely, and efficiently handle the client's job

Think of it as a business card, or a calling card, that you can show people no matter how far away they are from you.

A Note on "Freelancer"

Despite it being in the title of this book, I tend to recommend against using the word *"freelancer"* or *"freelance"* anywhere in your resume or bio. To a client, a freelancer sounds like someone who might not be around in a few months. I would recommend using something like *"translation professional"* or *"professional translator"* as your title, and to just refer to yourself as a translator, rather than a freelancer. This gives you a more professional air.

Some of you may be worried that recruiters are specifically targeting freelancers, and might be intimidated by the term *"translator"*. However, if they are finding you on ProZ or Translatorscafe, they already know more or less what you are. Most recruiters are only iffy about dealing with agencies, since they see an extra middleman cost there. Most of them won't consciously register a difference between *"translation professional"* and *"freelance translator"*, but it will just give a subconscious boost to your standing.

Getting Paid

(30 minutes – a couple days for approval, but you can start working in the meantime)

Bank Account

I am assuming all of you have this, if for no other reason than to connect to PayPal. I would not connect this directly to any other account, at least at the beginning, unless you have to. Using PayPal as a buffer tends to be safer. Keep in mind that all the websites I list here are legitimate and should be safe to connect to whatever bank account you like. However, I prefer to know that all my transactions have to go through a buffer before getting access to my personal account.

PayPal

There are several ways to get paid for your freelance work, but chances are that PayPal will be your end-all. It can link to your freelancer.com and Upwork accounts, and it can also then link to your bank account when you actually want to access your money. Most clients seem to prefer it as well.

A PayPal account can be set up quickly. It normally takes a few days to get your account approved and linked to your bank account. But in the meantime, you can start working, so don't worry about it. Just make sure you choose a personal account and fill out all your information truthfully. If there are any mistakes or discrepancies with your information, PayPal can be quite ruthless in its account-closing and blocking. The last thing you want is to have to contact their help department to access your money.

Keep in mind that PayPal charges you for business transactions ($0.30 USD plus a 2.9% transaction fee as of this writing). So you do have other options. The main one is:

Skrill

This used to be called Moneybookers, and you will find it referred to by either name. Skrill actually charges less than PayPal, (EUR 0.50 plus a

1.45% transaction fee as of this writing). Until recently, however, you could not use a United States bank account to sign up, so if you translate into or from English, chances are that your clients will prefer PayPal. Still now, there is a limit to the number of countries from which, and to which, you can send money (and these are two different lists). Feel free to check out or sign up for both, but for now I recommend concentrating on PayPal.

Transferwise

Transferwise is my preferred option for sending money internationally. Especially when you're dealing with substantial amounts, Transferwise seems to have the cheapest options, even beating bank-to-bank transactions. The one downside is that transactions can take a while. The company seems to wait until they receive a substantial amount to be transferred between the two countries and then execute all the transfers simultaneously. This is probably how they keep their fees low. Regardless, I use Transferwise to transfer money between my accounts in the United States and Europe, so feel free to check it out.

Setting up Your Account on Freelancer Websites
(1 hour max. per website)

You have a couple options for setting up an account on the various freelance websites. Some are free, some require payment, and some are free until you actually want to bid for a job. Some have a guaranteed escrow payment and some don't. Some will help you in case of non-payment, whereas some won't. And some will have decent jobs but others won't.

Plainly speaking, some are worth it and some aren't. This can also depend on what you're looking for so I will go through each of them here. The main issue at the beginning, however, is you don't know which ones are worth it and which ones aren't, so I suggest taking the time to create profiles for all of them. When it comes to paying for their services, you can take a minute and evaluate each of them one by one. In the meantime, just be present in as many places as you can.

Upwork.com

If you want a video walk-through of how to sign up for Upwork.com, you can go to this url: https://www.youtube.com/watch?v=Nd0aVVm9U EY

This website is a combination of what was once Elance.com and Odesk.com. The merger makes sense, since both these websites did pretty much the same thing. It is free to join and it covers all types of freelancing jobs, not just translations.

Simply go to Upwork.com and click on *"Signup"* in the top right corner. This will present you with the following screen:

Get your free account

First name	Last name

✉ Work email address

Sign Up with Email

Once you click *"Sign Up with Email"*, you'll land on another screen, where you should choose *"Work as a Freelancer"*. Fill out a username and password, and then verify your email.

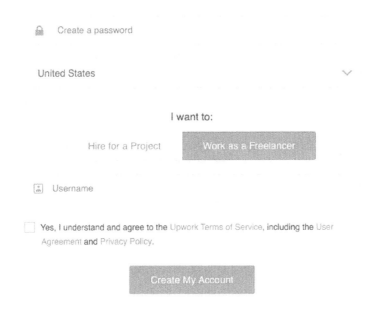

At this point, you can start to build your profile using all the information you prepared in the *"Pregame"* chapter. If you prepared all the information, it should pretty much be a matter of copying and pasting the correct text into the appropriate text boxes.

Once your profile has been built, you will have the option to take a placement test. Wait for this until your mind is fresh and you're alert. If you've been collecting your information and building your profile all this time, chances are you aren't in the best state of mind for a placement test, no matter how easy you think it's going to be. **Just wait until the next morning and tackle it when you your mind is well rested.**

freelancer.com

This is another website that has been gaining in popularity. Initially from Australia, it is now worldwide. One thing to keep in mind though is that freelancer.com does not have its own form of escrow. This means that there is a chance that you complete the work, send it off to the client and never hear from that client again. So make sure you use good judgment when dealing with clients. Having someone cheat you is pretty much a rite of passage for long-term translators. You just want to make sure it's never going to be a large job. In fact, simply aim to avoid the job altogether if it doesn't feel right. So, how do you avoid being scammed? Well, in addition to using your judgment, you can also check out the chapter *"Getting Paid,"* where I explain more on how you can cover your bases.

Other Websites

I will just group the other websites in this section because they can vary, depending on your language and country of residence. For example, machdudas.de is a website you will want to sign up for if you translate to or from German while addlance.com is a website all Italian translators should probably sign up for. The main issue is that, besides there being as many websites as there are languages, these websites often change. So, rather than make a list that will probably be outdated by the time you read it, I suggest you perform several searches (use both Google and Bing, just in case) for *"freelance translation"* and *"find translators"* in your language of interest. Remember, your potential client probably knows less than you do, so try to picture what they would type and how they would go about searching for a translator.

As an example, if I type *"Trova traduttori"* (*"find translators"* in Italian), the first result I get is addlance.com. This means a potential client is likely to do the same when looking for a translator like me. Therefore, if I perform Italian translations, I will probably want to sign up here.

"Trova traduttori"   🎤 🔍

Trova Traduttori Freelance - AddLance.com
https://www.addlance.com › Servizi ▾ Translate this page
★★★★★ Rating: 4.9 - 7,296 reviews
Solo su AddLance trovi inglese di traduttori italiani. Siamo esperti di qualsiasi lingua dal cinese all'arabo.

Trova traduttori inglese vicino a te - StarOfService
https://www.starofservice.sm › traduzione-inglese - Translate this page
Trova traduttori inglese in tutto il Paese. %%prosCount%% traduttori inglese trovati vicino a te.
Vai. Come funziona StarOfService. Rispondi a qualche domanda.

Atti e memorie - Accademia Virgiliana di Mantova
https://books.google.ch › books - Translate this page
Reale Accademia virgiliana di scienze, lettere ed arti - 1885 - Science
Nè la rovina della scolastica involge con sè la sorte del classico libro : esso trova traduttori e
lodatori tra gli Umanisti ed i Riformati, Leonardo Bruni nella prima ...

Atti e memorie - Page 221 - Google Books Result
https://books.google.ch › books - Translate this page
1884
Nè la rovina della scolastica involge con sè la sorte del classico libro : esso trova traduttori e
lodatori tra gli Umanisti ed i Riformati, Leonardo Bruni nella prima ...

Traduci il software sulla tua infrastruttura.
https://phrase.com › on-premise ▾ Translate this page
Le soluzione di gestione delle traduzioni sul proprio hardware dietro il firewall aziendale.
Collabora con il tuo team, trova traduttori professionisti e resta al top ...

Trova traduttori | TM-Town
https://www.tm-town.com › translators ▾ Translate this page

40

Setting up Your Account on Translation Websites
(1 hour max. per website)

ProZ.com

━━━

If you want a video walk-through of how to sign up for ProZ.com, you can go to this url: https://www.youtube.com/watch?v=qU_-2Vj4NfA

━━━

Okay, now we're dealing with a real translation website. In fact, this is the best translation site out there. Pretty much all serious translators either use this website or have used it on their way up, and will likely still have an active account. Unfortunately, the website is pretty cluttered, and it isn't the most intuitive, so you might want to take some time to navigate around and get familiar with it. I've been using it for close to ten years now and I still get annoyed at how it is structured.

So, the first thing will be to click on *"Are you a freelancer?"*, and then pick the free option. There is a catch though. You can sign up for free, but if you want to apply for jobs, you'll either have to purchase one of the memberships, or pay for each job you apply for. I suggest just purchasing the yearly membership, since in the long term it is usually worth it. But for now, you can just use the free option to sign up and enter all your information. You can then make the purchase decision later on.

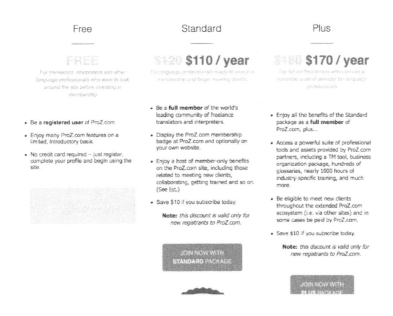

Free

Standard

Plus

FREE

~~$120~~ **$110 / year**

~~$180~~ **$170 / year**

For translators, interpreters and other language professionals who want to look around the site before investing in membership

For language professionals ready to invest in membership and begin meeting clients

For full-on freelancers who can use a complete suite of services for language professionals

- Be a **registered user** of ProZ.com

- Enjoy many ProZ.com features on a limited, introductory basis.

- No credit card required -- just register, complete your profile and begin using the site.

- Be a **full member** of the world's leading community of freelance translators and interpreters.

- Display the ProZ.com membership badge at ProZ.com and optionally on your own website.

- Enjoy a host of member-only benefits on the ProZ.com site, including those related to meeting new clients, collaborating, getting trained and so on. (See list.)

- Save $10 if you subscribe today.

   Note: *this discount is valid only for new registrants to ProZ.com.*

- Enjoy all the benefits of the Standard package as a **full member** of ProZ.com, plus...

- Access a powerful suite of professional tools and assets provided by ProZ.com partners, including a TM tool, business organization package, hundreds of glossaries, nearly 1000 hours of industry-specific training, and much more.

- Be eligible to meet new clients throughout the extended ProZ.com ecosystem (i.e. via other sites) and in some cases be paid by ProZ.com.

- Save $10 if you subscribe today.

   Note: *this discount is valid only for new registrants to ProZ.com.*

JOIN NOW WITH **STANDARD** PACKAGE

JOIN NOW WITH **PLUS** PACKAGE

Now just use all the information you have at hand from the *"Pregame"* section. You can also go ahead and set up your job notifications alert, by going to http://www.ProZ.com/dashboard/jobs. The beauty of this is that, instead of having to keep up with new jobs, you can simply have them delivered directly by email.

Now, in terms of the type of membership, you can evaluate them at http://www.ProZ.com/membership/. The types of membership, as of late 2019, have been whittled down to three: Free, Standard and Plus. The Standard is $110 per year, while the Plus is $170 (at the time of writing). You could of course decide not to pay and just remain a free user. However, the main downside of this is that you often won't have access to the same jobs as those of paying users. Most jobs are available only to paid users, at least for the first 12 hours. And even though you'll have access to them, you simply won't be able to apply to them without a fee. Also, you won't have full access to the Blue Board (I'll explain the Blue Board later).

Let me put it this way: in my opinion, if you need to decide if and where you should fork out money, then it should be this website. In terms of membership type, the Standard is more than enough when you're starting out as it gives you immediate access to all jobs in your language combinations, as well as to the Blue Board.

ProZ.com - Blue Board

"What is the Blue Board?", you ask? I'm glad you asked. When you look at potential job posts on the website, you will find that information about the company posting the job is at the bottom of the page, along with a link to the company's Blue Board account. This is where other translators who have previously worked with the company provide their feedback, so it's always useful to check this board before deciding whether to do business with them. Also, remember to check a broad range of comments. If someone gave a low score to a client, it could just as easily be due to a bad translator as it could be a bad provider. In general, however, people try to avoid giving bad reviews, so when you see one, treat it in general as a red flag.

About the outsourcer:

This job was posted by a Blue Board outsourcer with a "likelihood of working again" average rating of **5** out of 5

Note: You cannot quote because the quoting deadline has passed.

Once you have access to the Blue Board, it is actually a great resource for jobs in general. Any time you receive a request from any company dealing with translations, chances are they will be listed here, so you can search for them at http://www.ProZ.com/blueboard/.

ProZ.com – Other things

When you are set up, there are just a couple other factors to keep in mind. Hover over your name at the top, and you will see a long list appear (I told you this site can get a bit complicated). The first important link here is the one for **KudoZ points**, which you get by answering questions posted by others in your language combination. Basically, if you go to ProZ.com, you see job offers in your combination, and if you scroll down, you will see questions asked. Needless to say, this is a great place to ask any questions you may have. Bear in mind that you won't get any points for asking the questions, only for answering them.

The other point is what is called the **WWA**, or Willingness to Work Again. You can only get these points for jobs you have completed, so be sure to keep track of all your clients. Once you have completed a job to their satisfaction, you can simply ask them to give you feedback. ProZ.com makes it quite easy for you to send them a link with almost all the pre-filled information, and they're free to add their own information, should they wish. So be sure to collect these once you get started.

Recently ProZ.com also allowed clients to give you a rating. Of course, if you don't think they were happy with your work, you probably wouldn't ask them for a rating regardless, but just keep this in mind all the same. You don't want to risk a client giving you a poor score that then gets featured on your profile.

Another recommendation I have is the following link: https://www.proz.com/professional-guidelines/. Just read through these and then endorse the ProZ.com guidelines. These give you a good broad overview of what is expected of you and what you can expect from others. It also shows up on your profile that you adhere to these guidelines, which is always a help.

And while you are at it, you can also visit https://www.proz.com/securepro/security-practices/list and read through their list of safety practices. As you go through agreeing to these practices, they'll start to show up on your profile as well. Keep in mind though that you aren't required to agree to any of these.

Translatorscafe.com

This is the only other website that is more or less ubiquitous in the freelance translation world. Unfortunately, it isn't any more user-friendly than ProZ.com. In fact, if any of you have hard core website development skills, you might want to approach these companies and offer to simplify the user experience.

The initial process is pretty much the same as ProZ.com. Go to http://www.translatorscafe.com/cafe/EN/RegistrationQuest.asp where you can sign up as a linguist. Then, simply complete all your necessary information from the *"Before Getting Started"* chapter, as you did before.

This time however I would recommend remaining a non-paying member. You will still be able to see job requests and even apply for them, although you will receive some of them after everyone else, which can put you at a disadvantage. If after a month or so and you think it's worth it (as in, you still haven't been able to attract any responses and you're not busy working on jobs from other sources), then you certainly can upgrade. The good thing is that this website has only one paid membership option. This makes your life easier, since you just need to decide on the duration of membership. I recommend that you just sign up for the full year, if you can. Things like this can take time, so you might as well. You can do so by going to

http://www.translatorscafe.com/cafe/Upgrade.asp?T
ID=215630 and choosing your option.

Other Benefits of being a paid member include:

- Top placement of your name in search results
- Higher profile exposure
- Time saved through the use of some software
- Access to the hall of fame and shame

As you can see, these are nice, but they're not an absolute requirement. The site is geared more toward providing all they can for free, and paid membership is more for those who wish to support the website. At the time of writing, the cost for a yearly subscription is the same as ProZ.com, $110.

Other Websites

I was going to include translatorsbase.com in its own separate section, but I don't think it deserves that placement. Those who post jobs do not have to pay, while freelancers do. I've won some decent jobs from this website, but I've also been cheated on it (this website and freelancer.com are the only two that let me down in that sense). It's too easy for an ill-intentioned provider with a fake name to post a job for nothing using a yahoo.com email address and then disappear from the system without having to pay, once they have received the translation from some over-eager freelancer like me. And unfortunately, since translatorsbase.com does not keep the payment information of culprits like this, the company cannot do anything to help you.

How Not To Get Screwed Over By A Client

This is a real threat that all freelancers have to contend with. Some have created rules of thumb, such as never dealing with providers from a certain country, etc. At the end of the day, the best weapon is your head. Learning from other peoples' experience is invaluable as well. I have quite a bit of accumulated information about this, so check out the "Getting Paid" chapter for more. You will definitely want to read it through before accepting your first job.

There are some other translation websites as well, and they can be useful, depending on which language combination you specialize in, or which country you live in. Here is a list, which is by no means exhaustive. In fact, they may be more geared toward what I have experience in (Italian – English, with a smattering of some other European languages). If you have any other sites to recommend, feel free to let me know so I can add them to future editions of this book:

- traduguide.com
- guru.com
- workana.com *(this website always reminds me of Upwork.com, which is probably why it looks familiar)*
- addlance.com
- peopleperhour.com
- twago.com[2]
- machdudas.de
- translationdirectory.com
- translatorswork.com

Keep in mind also that some of these websites might just be aggregating job offers from other websites. I'm not exactly sure why they would do this unless they have an agreement in place with the

---

[2] I debated including this information, but thought I should for informational purposes: I have had serious issues with Twago's Safepay system. I tried withdrawing money from the account, and after several weeks I saw nothing in my bank account and nothing in my Twago account. So I contacted them (on two of their country websites). I was told the bank information was incorrect, although I had copied and pasted it from a past transaction, which had been successful. They then wrote: "Please consider that twago is not able to pay for any transaction fees or fees caused due to the bounce back (94,80€)." (SIC), which meant I had a 94.8 EUR (130 USD) fee charged to me. Again, this is anecdotal, but I thought I should include it nonetheless.

original website. Regardless, the result is a clogged-up inbox with multiple offers for the same job. The last thing you want is drowning a client's inbox with multiple copies of your resume. An example of this is http://www.etranslators.net/, which features various jobs that, when clicked on, link right back to translatorsbase.com.

What About Fiverr.com?

I may as well discuss fiverr.com, since chances are you've heard of it or seen the ads all over YouTube. I simply do NOT recommend fiverr.com as the site just isn't geared toward translation. Rather than people posting jobs and letting translators apply, people will pick providers and assign jobs to them right away. While this may work well with creative and/or long-term endeavors, it isn't really applicable to most translations, since you cannot gauge and assess which jobs to accept and what to charge for them ahead of time.

By the way, although you didn't ask, I never really recommend using fiverr.com. I can't think of any job I've truly been happy with through that website, despite the low price.

Direct Recruitment by Translation Agencies

Sooner or later, you will be contacted by translation agencies to become a member, most likely via one of these websites you've signed up for. In general, it is a good idea to sign up for them all, since you may as well have your information in as many places as possible.

Some of these sites may ask you to perform a short translation test for evaluation. In general, these tests should not be longer than 200-300 words. If they are longer, beware! They may just be trying to score a free translation off you. Yes, it happens, although thankfully it's rare.

I wouldn't expect too much from these sites. Many of them win clients by being able to claim they have X number of translators in their database. So, when they collect your information, they're just essentially beefing up their database. Whether or not you hear from them is another matter[3]. I seriously doubt they're in touch with even one hundredth of

---

[3] I've seriously spoken to agencies boasting about how they had 23,000 freelance translators in their database. Obviously, this just means they had 23,000 people sign up on their website.

them. On the other hand, if and when they do receive a job request in your language combination, it is always better to be on their list than not to be.

Some agencies may ask you for your social security number or equivalent, which could understandably make you feel uncomfortable. Others may ask you to physically mail your information to them (yes, really). I would suggest politely ignoring these. There's really no use in wasting time and money, or even risking your identity being out there for no real return.

Also, needless to say, if they ask you to pay for membership, just skip it! This means they are in the business of collecting fees instead of finding you translation jobs. Once you pay, they will concentrate their efforts on finding more freelancers to pay, rather than finding you translations.

Dealing with Contracts

From time to time, an agency or end client might send you a contract to sign. Most contracts, in my experience, fall under two main categories: **NDA (Non-Disclosure Agreement) and an Employment contract**.

NDA's tend to be pretty straight forward. They will state that you are not allowed to share or discuss any information with others. Obviously read through the contract and make sure you actually follow it. Don't discuss the content (even with family members), and then you can sign it.

Employment contracts can come in all shapes and sizes. Most large firms, if they have a contract, have pretty standard contracts they will ask their translators to sign. Regardless, you should actually read through the contract and make sure you agree with their points.

If you agree with the entire contract but only find one or two small points you disagree with, remember that you can always cross out the sections you don't agree with and initial the changes. Of course, the client may not accept your changes, so keep in mind that you might risk losing a client. But it is definitely better to do that than to find yourself in trouble further down the line.

Of course, if the entire contract is troubling, then it might be worth reevaluating whether or not you want to work with this particular client. Maybe try doing some research into them, especially on ProZ.com's Blueboard!

Take an Awesomeness Break

Now you're set! You've set up your profile and you've announced yourself to the world as a freelance translator. Go celebrate with a beer and feel good about what you've accomplished before moving on. At this point, you have at least put yourself out there, which is more than most prospective translators have been able to do, and more than any translator would have done around 10 years ago. Agencies from anywhere in the world can find you, hire you, and most importantly, pay you.

But this is just the beginning and the next phase of your journey starts tomorrow. For now, kick back and take it easy. Life is good and it's about to get a lot better.

If you've got nothing else to do, here's a picture of me, taken by my wife on a trip we took to Gruyeres and Bern, while we were living in Lugano, Switzerland, although the black and white doesn't do it justice:

(Take a deep breath, relax, and then we can start the next section)

AN EXPLANATION AS TO WHAT IS GOING ON AROUND YOU AND WHAT YOU'LL PROBABLY COME ACROSS

Let's Take a Step Back with Some Theory

I label this section *"theory"* because it is precisely that. You could just as easily skip this section and go right onto the *"Starting Strategy"* if you don't wish to waste any time before starting. But I consider it a worthwhile investment to read through this section, and to keep it as a handy reference guide. It will give you a good overview of the translation world and what to expect.

In this chapter, I will address some issues and terms that you've probably come across and aren't too sure about. First of all, you've probably heard of translation agencies and end clients. Let's start by addressing the various types of clients you may encounter.

Translation Agencies

We briefly touched upon this earlier, and in essence translation agencies are pretty self-explanatory – they're agencies that handle translation. But let's go into this a bit more in detail.

First of all, there are all sorts of agencies. If you've have a good or bad experience with a certain agency, this doesn't mean that the next agency will

60

necessarily be a good or bad one. Most agencies these days offer various types of translations, usually in multiple languages. Some may specialize in certain types of languages, such as European, Asian, African, etc., while others specialize in certain industries, such as medical, legal, financial, etc.

Most agencies these days work with freelance translators (like you) rather than in-house translators. And it's obvious why. It costs them less and it gives them access to worldwide talent. Of course, this also means that merely being on an agency's database doesn't really mean much. Plenty of agencies have tens of thousands of translators in their databases, but will only actually communicate with a very small minority of them.

However, agencies also handle all the headache of finding end clients who need translations. This spares you the trouble of having to do that job yourself.

∙∙∙

Picture this: You are an English-Korean translator. ABC Widgets is an American company that wants to expand to Asia, but doesn't know how, so they hire someone to manage this project. This new person they hired will be responsible for finding new contacts, maybe a local distributor, as well as potential new clients. In addition, they'll need to locate an importer, some people to deal with widget regulations in each local market and translators for converting their marketing material into the local language. Since translation is just one part of their requirements (and they'll need translation in five different languages), they'll need to find an agency to handle everything. The agency can basically hold their hand, explaining what needs to be translated and what doesn't: *"Don't worry, people in Singapore will understand English, but you need to change your currencies and shipping info!"*

This agency can then hire various translators, and you, as a Korean-English translator, will handle a portion of this big job. This makes your life easier, since you can just concentrate on the translation instead of the other issues, and you don't need to worry about business development trying to grow your business as much either. But this also means that the agency will get paid more than you do.

Some things to keep in mind when dealing with agencies:

- They should not charge to register on their database. *As I outlined earlier, professional agencies don't do this.*
- They should pay you for your work, regardless of whether or not they are paid by the end client. *Your contract is with the agency, not the end client. So you shouldn't have to pay for their issues.*

- You can charge extra for more work. *For example, if the agency requires formatting or something else in addition to translation, you're be free to charge more or to emphasize that you're a translator and formatting is technically outside your remit.*

Some tricks agencies may try to pull:

It's rare that agencies pull these kinds of stunts, but you should at least be aware of them.

- The agency hires a good translator to complete a short demo translation during the bidding process for a job by an end client. Then, once the agency wins the job, they might hire another cheaper translator who's not as good to handle the full job.

- The agency might try to hire only students and offer to compensate them with a recommendation letter, the promise of a future reference, or abysmally low fees.
- You might be hired by an agency to edit a text that has already been translated, but then you find out that the agency has simply run the text through Google Translate or Bing Translate. This way they only have to pay for editing fees, rather than translator fees. *Keep in mind that an agency might even be upfront about this ("post-editing machine translation"), and some agencies might even try to pass their machine translation off as human (I once caught a prospective client doing this).*

Are Translation Agencies My Clients or Not?

You may have noticed that most people searching for translators actually work for translation agencies. So what is going on here? Well, most end clients end up contacting a translation agency who will then contact you to carry out the actual translation. This means translation agencies act as *"middlemen"*, but they also serve a purpose.

First of all, they are a buffer in between you and the end client. For example, if the end client doesn't pay them, the agency still owes you payment for your work. Secondly, it is up to the agency to interpret what the client wants, since the end client likely may have no idea what a source word is, or what the difference between Simplified and Traditional Chinese is. It's also likely that a lot of other work is going into the job. For example, in additional to hiring agency for a translation job of a presentation into four languages, a client may also need the documents to be reformatted. Or the numbers might need to be updated. Or the documents might need to be compatible for certain computer systems.

I therefore recommend you work through a translation agency in the beginning. Once you become more comfortable, you may want to start actively targeting end clients. While they will require more handholding and explanation, they will also pay much more, and often in advance. So keep this in mind as a medium or long-term goal.

Direct Clients

Direct clients are the "*end*" clients who need the translation done in the first place. As described above, this can mean a lot more handholding, but you're also getting paid a lot more.

You will need to **be careful about talking with direct clients**. Chances are they have no idea what a source language is, what machine translation means, or even what the difference between translation and interpreting is. They are hiring you to handle all that, so make sure everything is clear.

Ensure you understand exactly what they need as an end product. You don't need to tell them the details of how you will handle the work, but confirm they are asking for the right thing. For example, *do they really need translation in traditional Chinese, or did they mean simplified Chinese? Do they really need this certificate to be translated or is it a different one? If they translate this contract, does* *that mean that all past contracts need to be translated as well? Etc. etc.*

You will also need to guide the direct client in terms of **timelines and expectations**. They may not know how long it takes to complete a translation or, for that matter, realize for example that translating a document from English to Arabic might require a lot of reformatting: in one version, the reader reads roman letters from left to right, while in the other version, the reader's eyes move from right to left and the writing may take up more (or less) space.

Also keep in mind that you'll be bearing the **risk of non-payment**. So make sure you can handle these matters as well. Do you want to get paid up-front? In multiple installments? In which currency? Will you charge interest for late payments? What about VAT?

Individuals

Individuals, while also direct clients, tend to generally require different services. You will usually be hired by an individual for the translation of a birth certificate, some personal documentation, or school records, etc. Some may also want to hire you to translate a thesis or dissertation or perhaps even edit it.

67

If you are translating official documents, check to see whether they require certification or notarization. And look over precisely what the work entails. It often differs for each country, and sometimes even for different regions within a country.

It is generally advisable to charge a set price per document in advance. As a reference, many online services will translate legal documents such as a birth certificate for $25 per page, including certification.

Some translators consider these documents a pain, and decline this type of work. Others like them, since they tend to all be similar after a while. So feel free to try a couple of documents and see how it works out. A translator I know works closely with his country's consular office and handles all of their documentation. It's a really simple way for him to earn money.

Does Google Translate Mean We Won't Have a Job in a Few Years?

In short: No. We'll be fine. In fact, the global freelance translation market is growing every year, shows no sign of slowing down, and is on track to hit a market value of $56 billion by the year 2021[4]. The fact is, no matter how much improvement we see with Google Translate and other machine translation tools, most financial firms, banks, law firms, and basically all corporations will continue to use real translators. Why is this?

The truth is that Google Translate still makes plenty of mistakes, and you absolutely cannot afford to risk this in important documents such as legal contracts or financial statements.

But a much more important issue is the mechanism used by Google Translate itself. **It actually doesn't translate anything**! Instead, it scours the web for similar or identical translations performed in the past, constantly learning and building upon what it has learned. This might sound great, but this also means that any time you plug in a word, phrase or paragraph or upload a document

---

[4] https://www.statista.com/statistics/257656/size-of-the-global-language-services-market/

into Google Translate, you are effectively granting Google *"a worldwide license to use, host, store, reproduce, modify, create derivative works (such as those resulting from translations...)"*[5]. As you can imagine, most corporations (and law firms) aren't too keen on this. And remember, this happens regardless of whether you are logged into Google or not. *You can read more about Google's policies here: https://policies.google.com.*

Of course, this doesn't mean we should ignore machine translation. Being in the industry, it's our duty to keep track of technology and of the changes taking place in the translation world. In fact, many of these changes can be of great benefit to those who use them correctly. So don't worry too much about Google Translate. Just keep track of it (and other types of technology).

---

[5] https://policies.google.com/terms?hl=en-US#toc-content

What about Interpreting? Isn't That Translation?

Well, not really. Many people, even clients, may ask for translation when they actually mean interpreting. I find this happens most often in English speaking scenarios where *"translation"* is loosely used for *"interpreting"* (but not vice versa). Regardless, this doesn't mean that you should make the same mistake. Translation refers to the translation of a *written text* from one language to another. Interpreting on the other hand refers to the translation of the *spoken word* and translating it into another spoken language.

This book only covers written translations. I am a translator and work solely with translators, so this is the only area I feel qualified to discuss. However, if you are a freelance interpreter, hopefully many of these points can apply as well. In case you are interested, I can give a very brief introduction to interpreting here below:

---

[6] Definitions taken from the European Commission terminology page:
https://ec.europa.eu/info/departments/interpretation/conference-interpreting-types-and-terminology_en

Types of Interpreting

First of all, there are three main types of interpreting[6]:

- **Consecutive**: Interpreting takes place after the speaker has finished, usually with the help of notes.
- **Simultaneous**: Interpreting occurs while the person is speaking with the aid of equipment such as booths, earphones, and/or microphone.
- **Whispered or Chuchotage**: The interpreter is seated or standing with the participants and interprets simultaneously directly into their ear.

Another Thing to Keep in Mind

If you are planning on becoming an interpreter, you should keep in mind that the language combination is the opposite when compared to translation. While I outlined earlier in this book that translators always translate INTO their native language, *interpreters should always translate FROM their* **native language** into their target or "*active*" language. This is so they're able to pick up on subtle inferences and tones that a native speaker

72

might not pick up on. Of course, it might be difficult to translate a joke or some type of innuendo, but at least recognizing it for what it is can help a great deal. I've seen many interpreters deal with jokes by simply saying something like *"that was such a dirty joke, I'm not even going to translate it"*.

DESCRIBING SOME APPROACHES YOU CAN TAKE AND WHY

Starting Strategy

Legalities

Before actually starting out, we should address legal issues. This is something that many people find concerning, and with good reason. Unfortunately, there is no set answer, since it will depend on which country you live in, and often which region of the country you live in, as well as which country your clients might be in. The legalities can also change over time, so even if I give you information that is correct at the time of writing, the legalities may have changed again by the time you read this.

That said, you cannot simply ignore the legalities of getting into business. So, let's start off by emphasizing that I'm NEITHER a lawyer, NOR do I have any legal training, so I ask you not to assume that my advice has any legal standing. Along those lines, I advise you to get in contact with someone who is trained in the legal profession who also lives in your region. Preferably, you'll want a lawyer who deals with entrepreneurs, startups, and/or freelancers. And if you're lucky, this *lawyer can give you some tax advice as well, alongside your accountant.* Although this might cost you money, you can usually limit it to one meeting in order to obtain the correct information, and it can help you rest easy as you proceed with your job.

Another thing you can do is to talk to other people in your shoes. In other words, **find other freelancers and entrepreneurs in your same area**. Chances are they'll have had to deal with the same issues, and they may even be able to recommend a good lawyer and/or accountant to help out with these issues.

You can also do an online search. Be aware of the potential issue that A) the information you find might be outdated, since laws can change quite often, and B) the information might not be precisely relevant to your exact situation.

Just as I am not a lawyer, chances are that you aren't one either. So while you think you're searching for the correct terms, it might turn out that, legally speaking, completely different terms are being used for people in your situation and completely different laws will apply.

By the way, pretty much the same as above will apply to tax issues. So make sure to ask about these when you talk to the lawyer as well. While accountants typically handle tax issues, the lawyers can usually at least steer you in the right direction. They may also let you know if you don't really need an accountant yet.

Your Strategies

Now it's time for phase two of your strategy, which is actually actively getting your name in front of the right people. Here I will discuss **how to be up to date** on the job offers out there, **how to push your name and information** out in front of the providers, **how to increase your chances of actually being chosen** for any job, as well as how to increase your chances of **repeat business**.

Your System

Before we get into the nitty gritty, it's worth mentioning that from an admin perspective you should always give the impression that you're already invoicing 20 regular clients, even though you may only be starting out with 1 or 2 clients.

In other words, you don't want to start with an ad hoc system and then improve as you go along, because you'll simply have to do extra clean up later further down the line. It might be impossible to remember what job was performed for which client, where you saved the files, who paid you and who hasn't yet, and all while keeping track of all your current job deadlines.

Alerts

Hopefully, you have set up job alerts wherever possible on websites such as ProZ.com and translatorscafe.com. Some websites, however, may not offer this option. I find that in these situations you will tend to sporadically check their websites for a few days, and then sooner or later, you'll forget to check in as often. And that's when the chances of missing out on some opportunities happen.

The easiest option here is to set up regular **alerts on Google Calendar,** or another suitable calendar you use regularly. I'll usually check my language combination on the website and then look at the dates of the postings. Then, depending on their frequency, I will set up an alert for every Monday/Wednesday/Friday, once per week, or once per month.

Your Calendar

While we are on the subject of calendars, it is important not to take yours lightly. I've spoken to a number of people who, when starting out, set up an entire new calendar for work**. I do not recommend this**. I think it's best to have just one. You don't want to risk being at the doctor's scheduling your next appointment for 3 months down the line, and then a week before the appointment date, you hear back from a client and schedule a meeting for the same time because you are in front of a different calendar. Google calendar works great for me because I can keep personal and business on the same calendar, just in different colors, and I can get an alert the day before an event. This way I can be sure not to schedule a client meeting when I have a personal appointment and vice-versa.

Pricing

At the beginning, you will find that ratings and reviews are just as important, if not more important, than prices. The job providers won't want to hire someone totally new, so you may have to suffer a bit at the beginning. Many established freelance translators will be mad at my recommendation here, but I do recommend **underpricing** yourself, at least in the beginning. There are, of course, some downsides to this:

- You will earn less.
- The hiring company will expect the same price for all future translations.

- Other translators will lose out due to your underpricing.

Other freelancers may claim that this makes you look inexperienced. I disagree on the basis that if you're a first-time translator on any website, you'll look inexperienced regardless. Therefore, gaining some valuable experience, a track record, and some money is better than not getting hired due to misplaced pride.

The main reason that many freelancers balk at this is that it underprices the entire industry, or so they claim. I simply don't agree with this. There will always be extremely low-priced translators. The ones that are worth it will naturally be able to command more over time. On the other hand, the new ones will have to start somewhere. When I first started, I was told by several people to never go below $0.10 USD per source word, since that was what I was worth. But the result of this strategy was not winning a single job in over five months. I finally became desperate, starting accepting ridiculously low-priced jobs, and started making money. You can often even tell the client that you will accept their low rate as long as they provide good feedback for you, since you're trying to create a track record. I think you will find most providers will be happy to save money if all it costs them is a five-star rating (as long as they're happy with your work, of course).

Working for Free

As I am writing the 3rd edition of this book, I think that the option of working for free deserves its own section. In fact, I almost decided to delete the underpricing section in favor of this one. How come? Well, working for free is both more effective and less damaging in the long-term than underpricing.

When first starting out, your ratings and reviews can be leveraged for winning future jobs. What does this mean? Well, in essence, when you are assigned a job, you can ask for a rating once you've successfully completed the assignment. Platforms like Upwork.com or Translatorscafe.com provide a star rating system, and on ProZ.com, this is known as the WWA. These ratings provide tremendous value over the long-term. When prospective clients wish to hire a translator, seeing ratings and reviews by previous clients is probably the single most important factor they take into account. You can take this from someone running his own agency.

So, when applying for a job, why not say something like *"As you can see, I am just starting out, so I am willing to perform this job for free for you.*

In exchange all I ask is that you leave me a good review, if you are satisfied with my work." I don't know many people who will refuse a free service, and as long as you do a good job, you are pretty much guaranteed a great review.

Of course, since you won't be earning anything from this job, it might best to limit your non-earning assignments to the small jobs. But an advantage it has over underpricing yourself is that it doesn't pigeon-hole you in a certain price range, which is what happens when you decide to charge a very cheap price just to get your first clients.

Hold On. How Does Pricing Work?

At this point you might be wondering how to price your work. Per word? Per page? Per line? Per hour? Per project? Per cups of coffee? Well, the standard in the industry is **per source word**, but let's give all the strategies a brief overview:

Pricing Strategy One: Per Source Word

When starting out, I would always try to give a price per source word, or precisely, per word of the source text. This ensures that you get paid for the work you actually perform. In contrast, being paid per hour will always be more of an art than a science, and charging by the page can also be a challenge, since some pages can consist of just a header, whereas others might contain small text with very wide margins. Charging per word, on the other hand, ensures that you get paid for what you translate.

The reason I specify a price per source word (i.e. per word of the source text) rather than per target word (per word of the text after you have translated it) is so that both you and the client can know ahead of time what the precise price will be. This also ensures the client that you won't be adding any unnecessary words in order to squeeze a bit more out of them.

Sometimes a client might ask for a quote per target word. This might happen for example if they've scanned a document and they don't know how to how to calculate the word count on a pdf document, which is fine. Depending on the language, variations between source and target word counts can vary by up to 30% with western languages, and even more with others. Next time you see a text that is translated into Chinese, compare the number of characters with the number of words! You can search forums for discussions about this based on language combinations. Or in a worst-case scenario you can seek out a certain number of past translations and see what the average difference in word count is.

Also, depending on which language combination or which countries you are dealing with, you may receive a request for a quote per ten words, per thousand words, or even per character or per line. While there are variations between languages, as a general rule of thumb I would say that there are **50-65 characters** (including spaces) **per line**, and **1,500 to 1,800 characters per page**.

Another thing to think about is your lowest rate, or your *"pain barrier"*, as one colleague calls it. This is the rate below which you will not work. This may change over time, but you should decide what it is. Rest assured, the moment will come when you will be asked to work for less.

How To Calculate Word Count

You should always know how to calculate the word count before getting started. This is good for double-checking the client's assertions, as well as being able to gauge your pricing for yourself.

<u>Using Microsoft Word</u>

If you're using Microsoft Word, the easiest option is to click on Tools -> Word count. Be sure you don't have any of the text highlighted at the time (so that it calculates the whole document), and be sure to check the box "include footnotes and endnotes"

Using any other program

Different programs have different methods but, if in doubt, just copy **all** the text and paste it into Microsoft Word, **and** then follow the same process as above.

What if it is a scanned document (or any other document that doesn't allow for word count)?

In this case, you will want to use what is called an Optical Character Recognition, or OCR. The one I use is http://www.onlineocr.net. There are other, free options, but I prefer to pay for their services. As of this writing, for $4.95 you can scan 50 pages, and it works pretty well. You can then download the scan in various formats, including Microsoft Word, after which you can repeat the steps above.

<u>But I don't have Microsoft Word...</u>

This might be a bigger problem than you think, especially if you receive translations that require a certain format. But for now, there are websites that calculate word counts. One of the main ones seems to be http://www.wordcounttool.com. Regardless of the one you use, however, just make sure to copy and paste all the text, rather than upload a document, since it guarantees a more precise count.

Pricing Strategy Two: Per Project

Once you get going, another option will start to make more sense, and this is charging per project. I mention this as a second option, because you can only really start doing this once you are used to the pitfalls that can arise. For example, a document of ten pages can mean very different things. Or a document of a thousand words could mean a scanned, barely legible copy of around thousand *handwritten* words. It could mean a thousand new words with four thousand repeats. Or it could be a thousand words of poetry, which can take much longer than a thousand words of a website's 'About Us' page.

But, if you know more or less what to expect, both from the document and the type of client, then you can start charging per project. The advantage of this is that the client will simply receive a straightforward and transparent price, instead of a tedious price calculation. Let's take the example of a document that contains 6,857 words. Rather than say your price per source word is $0.07 (which means you're leaving it to the client to calculate 6857 * $0.07 = $479.99 in order to see if it fits within the budget), you could just say you can finish the whole project for $480.

Once again, it's a relatively small step, but making their life that much easier can often be the push needed to winning the project. Bonus points if you can provide a fixed delivery date rather than a timeline. Bear in mind though that this might be risky, since they might wait two days before assigning the job to you. So you need to specify delivery date from the moment the client awards you the job. **In other words, don't say "I can finish this by September 28th", but "I can finish this within 4 days from confirmation".**

Not Recommended - Charging by the Hour

I thoroughly recommend either one of the above two strategies, but do not recommend pricing per hour. This is bad for you for several reasons:

1. There is a clear-cut ceiling rate for hours you can work in a day. There are only 24 hours in a day, so, if you charge per hour, you realize quite quickly that your earning potential is limited by the number of hours available. And I'm assuming you also want to eat and sleep.

2. There is also a clear-cut ceiling in your hourly rate. You could argue that you could raise your hourly rate. But there is only so much you can charge per hour. No one will hire a translator for USD 100 per hour. However, if you price your work correctly and become efficient, then you can certainly get paid that amount. This is also because, when a recruiter asks for an hourly rate, it becomes a race to the bottom. If the recruiter is comparing hourly rates, the topmost rates will automatically get cut, and, chances are, the decision will be made solely on the cheapest acceptable rate. And being in a race to the bottom is not a good race to be in.

3. There's no incentive for you to work efficiently. This is also bad for the company hiring you, although they often don't realize it. It means you have no incentive to finish your work quickly, and you have every incentive to drag it out as much as possible. **You end up selling your time rather than your work**, so you will become very good at finding ways to add time here and there. This is neither good for the client nor for you, since you could be using that time to do better work.

Aside from all this, charging by the hour, more often than not, just amounts to less. In fact, try doing the math. For example, how long does it take you to translate a thousand words? And what would you charge for that? Now, what hourly rate does that come out to? Is it more or less than what you can expect to charge per hour? Chances are, you would get paid more per hour by charging per word, regardless, so I would advise you to avoid charging per hour if at all possible.

Having said all this, the one exception I've noticed to this rule has been with editing. Sometimes, depending on the quality of the original translation, quite a bit of time might be required to edit the text. In this case it might be worth charging per hour, with the understanding that it will take you quite a bit of time to complete the job (usually at least a range is agreed upon in advance).

Price Minimum

The only other thing to keep in mind for the pricing section is your price minimum. Especially when you're starting out, you will want to have a minimum price. Sometimes translators want to skip the very short jobs (like, say, a driver's license or a birth certificate), because they might have 15 or 20 words, and are therefore not worth the time it takes to correspond with the client and accept the job. However, if you have a minimum price, then each one of these jobs can be an easy way to add some money. Obviously, your minimum can't be too high, so find the level you're most comfortable with.

Creating an Estimate for the client (Larger jobs)

Another way to appear more professional to the client is to send them "an estimate", rather than just a price quote. I only recommend this for larger, more involved projects and, if you can, find a way to paste it in the message, since many clients might not want to open attachments.

An estimate basically has the same information as a price quote, but is more professional looking, and can also include some more personalized details, should you wish them for larger projects. They tend to include:

Price

Refer to paragraphs above for pricing strategies, but, if this is a large job, you may also want to give a price per phase, and divide the large job into different phases

Scope

This just details what exactly you will perform (translation plus editing and reworking as needed, for example). The added benefit is that anything extra can get charged extra. So if they sneak in a new file, or ask for some formatting, you can add that on, since it is outside of the scope.

Rough timeline

I say rough, because you want to leave some leeway, in case they are late in sending you files, or changes need to be made, etc.

Deposit/payment terms

These can be the usual ones, although, if it's a large job, you can probably ask for partial payments along the way.

Expiration date of the offer

This is important too. Don't be stingy with this, but let them know that they can't get back to you in 6 months and say "Hey we want to hire you on those terms". This also makes sure you're not waiting forever for a job that might not happen.

That's All Great. But What Should I Charge?

Right about now is when frustrated translators tell me I keep talking and talking (or writing and writing), but never give an actual rate. Well, unfortunately it's almost impossible to give you an actual rate to charge, but let me at least give you some pointers to help you out:

Standard Rates

First of all, if you want to get an idea of what other people are charging, you can go to https://search.proz.com/employers/rates and enter your language combination (as well as the specialization) to see what the standard rates are. Of course, you don't have to charge these specific rates, and in my experience, translators will be proposing a wide variety of rates for individual jobs.

What If They Mention a Rate?

Often when companies post a job they will either mention a rate or a range that they are willing to pay. Once again, this will be a judgment call on your part, but it might be worth coming back to them on the higher side, and see if they negotiate. Or you could possible give them a rate above their range, and see how they respond. Of course, you also risk losing the client altogether, so be careful. Also keep in mind that agencies often don't have much leeway in what to pay their translators.

Work Backwards

It is also useful to work backwards. What I mean by this is that you should keep in mind how much you will have to earn in order to be making a living. So it might be useful to figure out your budget, see how much you will be required to earn per year, per month and per week, and this can give you an idea as to how much you will need to be earning.

This Can Depend on Specializations Too

In general, the more specialized the translation, the more you can charge. Then again, the more specialized you are, the fewer jobs you might win. This can also depend on the type of specialization. In general, medical texts will pay more than texts (even very technical ones) about art history. There are always exceptions, so, once again, it might be worth looking at comparisons on https://search.proz.com/employers/rates.

Am I Entitled to Payment?

This is a section I wish I didn't have to write, but unfortunately it will probably come up at some point. In essence it boils down to this: if you complete your job successfully according to the agreed upon parameters, you should get paid. Sounds sort of obvious, right? Unfortunately, issues come up all the time.

This has been mentioned before, but it is worth repeating. If the agency (or client) you are working with says they cannot pay you because they haven't received payment from their end client yet, this is not acceptable. Your contract is with the party who contracted you, not with their end client. This is their risk, not yours.

Then again, you may have made a mistake. If this is the case, it is best to offer to make as many corrections as needed. There are, of course, limits to this, and you will get the hang of it after a while. At the beginning, you can include something like this in your invoice:

"All translations can be reworked as much as required, should something not to be your satisfaction. Once 20 days have passed, the translation will be assumed to have been satisfactory and accepted."

You can obviously tweak this as needed, but at least it means they cannot contact you 6 months down the line asking you to rework a translation for free. This also means they cannot delay payment for that long.

Of course, they might find some mistakes, and correcting these mistakes creates more work for them. If this is the case, they may ask you for a discount. This will be a judgment call, but remember that a discount is better than no payment at all. If you believe they are not in the right then you can say so. I generally find that, if they are petty and try to get a discount when one wasn't warranted, I will try to fight it a bit, but not too much. I would rather receive my discounted fee and just never work for them again, chalking it up to a lesson learned.

- Before Getting Started

- Let's Take a Step Back with Some Theory

- Starting Strategy

- **Finding Clients**

- Marketing

- Good Problems: You've Won an Assignment. Now What?

- Getting Paid

- Other Tips and Tricks to Keep in Mind

- Next Steps

DISCUSSING WHO YOUR CLIENTS ARE, AND WHERE AND HOW TO FIND THEM

Finding Clients

It might seem weird that we are this far into the book before we actually set about finding clients. But, if you look back, there is a reason for this. The worst thing you could do is to actually find some prospective clients, only to find that you're ill-prepared, you don't have the right information, or you don't know how to price your work.

The good news is that once everything has been set up, you don't really need to worry about it again. You will be updating information as you go along, but all of the information up to this point only really needs to be covered once.

From now on, however, you will be rinsing and repeating quite a bit. By this I mean that you'll probably be spending most of your time finding new clients. In fact, I'll say this: **Please don't apply to 20 different companies and then complain to me that you can't find work!** Unfortunately, the search for new clients takes much more effort than that in the beginning. In fact, a major chunk of your time will be dedicated to winning new clients, with some breaks for translation here and there. That's a better way to look at it. Seriously. While I got a job here and there relatively quickly, it took me almost a year to find my first regular client, and even then, that was one regular client. To this day, I'm still working on my marketing and still reach out to prospective clients.

I will cover some basics for finding clients here, with a separate marketing section later on.

The Basics

I would recommend contacting at least ten prospects per week at the beginning, but feel free to raise that to 20 per week. The majority, at the beginning, will likely be agencies (in fact, I would concentrate solely on these at first), and the response rate will be very low. Of course, there is no set formula, and you can raise the response rate significantly by following certain steps (like those outlined in this book), but expect the response rate to be less than 10% in the beginning.

Later on, once you have steady work and more regular clients, you will dedicate less time to finding new clients, but it will never go away entirely. So this is an important section.

Some Places to Find Prospective Clients

I will assume that at the beginning, you will be targeting translation agencies rather than end clients.

In this case, some good places for finding clients will be:

- The American Translator's Association (ATA) website: https://www.atanet.org/
- A Translation association in the country of your other language *(e.g. if you translate to or from Italian, the "Associazione italiana traduttori e interpreti" is probably a good source)*
- Proz.com/blueboard
- Translatorscafe.com
- Google: [Your hometown] + "Translation agency"
- Google: [Your hometown] + *"Translation agency in your other language"*

How to Contact Agencies

In short: follow instructions! This means that you shouldn't try to be different or original. If an agency's website asks you to fill out a form, then that's what you should do. If they ask you to apply online, don't send a physical CV to their offices just to stand out. Remember, these agencies hear from dozens of translators per day. This means they have a system to find the translators they can work with. Usually this means filling out a form, or Excel sheet, or something along those lines, so they can then easily search for translators in the required language combinations.

This also means that **sending out blanket emails to random agencies is almost never a good idea**! The best case scenario is that the agency will politely ask you to fill out their online (or attached) form. But often your email address will get marked as spam.

So rather than wasting your time, go to the agency's website and click on their link for translators (they will pretty much always have one), and then follow the instructions.

Seriously, take it from someone who is now running an agency (even if it is a small one). An email from a prospective translator who can't follow simple instructions in applying for a job will be the easiest email to delete, especially if it's a blanket email that

103

is obviously copied and pasted to many different companies!

Alternative to Finding Clients: Finding Jobs!

When you're starting out you might find yourself applying for individual jobs rather than looking for new clients. I actually think this will be more effective than applying to agencies, but I wanted to mention the agencies first, since it doesn't hurt to send your information to as many places as possible.

Finding jobs means keeping track of jobs on websites like ProZ.com and Translatorscafe.com. But, once again, if you signed up for job alerts, this will pretty much be taken care of for you. So now you just need to apply for each job individually. Let's discuss how to go about that.

Personalized Introductions

After a potential client lists a potential job and hears back from translators, they will probably be sifting through 10-30 different offers. Here you will want to make sure that your introduction stands out for the right reasons. There are various ways of accomplishing this. Some recommend rewriting your introduction for each new job offer, but this is the quickest way to ensure that you will never want to apply to another job again, especially after your 20th application. Remember, if the clients are receiving 30 applications for every job offer, they will only choose one out of 30, so yes, you may send out 20 applications or more before hearing back from anyone.

On the other hand, you can't just copy and paste your same application to every new job, since this will guarantee that the potential client will send your application to the bottom of the heap. After all, if you aren't willing to put in the effort of applying, why should they bother putting in the effort of checking your credentials?

So, what is the solution? Well, as with anything else, it is to combine the better options of each choice.

Let's say, as in the example I mentioned in the first chapter, your main specializations are business and legal translations. In this case, I would set up three templates. One is for business translations, the other for legal, and the third for all other translations. Here is a generic example of a possible template for Italian-English legal translation offers and is a variation of what I used quite effectively for several years:

Hello NAME,

As an Italian-English translator, I would be happy to assist you with your LEGAL TRANSLATION.

My legal translation experience is extensive: from DOCUMENTS FOR THE COURT OF PADUA to contracts to legal correspondence.

I have published articles for Cornell University's The Current, was a columnist for The International Affairs Journal and have been published in the Swiss-Italian paper Corriere del Ticino.

Moreover, having been born to an Italian mother and an American father, and having grown up in both the United States and Italy, I am truly bilingual.

You can find more information, including

some sample translations, on my ProZ profile page
here: http://www.ProZ.com/profile/1494149.

My rate for this job would be EUR 0.07 per source word and I am ready to begin at your convenience. If you would like any further information, please do not hesitate to contact me.

Thank you,

Robert Gebhardt
http://about.me/robertgebhardt

The parts in red should be filled out specifically for each client. I tend to leave these in caps and in a different color for my templates, since it is a glaring, extremely obvious, reminder for me to fill these fields out. For each point:

1. If you don't have a name for the client, just write *"hello"*. Don't use the agency's name or, even worse, *"to whom it may concern"*.
2. The second red part should restate what the client wants, usually in the name of their request (such as "10 Page Court of Padua Judgment," or something like that). Once again, if there is no real usable name, just stick with *"legal translation"*.
3. The third red part should mention the job you've performed which is most similar to the one being requested.
4. The price per word may change, depending on various factors, such as the subject matter, the length, the type of document, the deadline, and obviously how desperate you are for work.

Notice how I then follow all this with what I think will be the most impressive part of my generic experience (describing how I am a published author in both languages).

I then entrench my credentials by stating I am fully bilingual, after which I try to establish the "trust" factor. I provide a link to my ProZ profile (yes, I use my ProZ profile even when replying to requests on other websites).

Only toward the end do I state my rate, followed by a polite salutation. *"Best Regards"* has no meaning, and everyone pretty much knows that. Then I add another factor of trust at the very end, with a link to my about.me website (as of the 3rd edition of this book, I would change this to whatever your mail profile page is, even if you are repeating a ProZ.com profile page from earlier).

This is, of course, only a template to be used as an example. I post it up here because it has worked quite well for me. You will have your own strengths, and you may even have a better way of stating them. The main point I want to emphasize here is to have a reason for everything you state in your introduction. A good way of doing this is to be able to give a reason for each sentence you write. Ask yourself, *"Does this phrase add anything that hasn't already been stated? If so, is it something that will make the client more likely to hire me?"*

Also, keep in mind that it can be as personalized as you wish. The only limit is how much time you wish to dedicate to it. In other words, you can have several templates for various types of legal translations. Or you can send some samples to potential clients, even without their having requested them. You could even send pictures if you imagine they would support your application. Or, if someone says they need a precise translation you can add that you are meticulous and have great attention to detail. And so on.

Personalized Bios

Many websites come with their own bio templates, where you can just fill in the blanks. I highly recommend NOT using these. Also, don't use bio and introduction examples that you find online. Remember that many other translators are following the same steps you are, and the best way to blend in with the crowd, look like you put in very little effort, and be forgotten, is to sound like everyone else.

I'm not saying you should have some weird, eye-catching slogan just to stand out. You want to come across as serious, not totally different. But you do want to stand out at least enough for them to remember you. Use your own words. You can use any pre-written bio, including the one I provided above as a starting point. Just make sure your final piece of work is different enough so as not to be recognizable.

Other Questions to Ask Regarding Specific Jobs

If you have made an initial contact with the client, you might want to be clear about what you're getting into before accepting their translation assignment. So don't be afraid to ask questions like:

- How many words, or pages?
- What is the deadline?
- Can I see the document, or an extract, before starting?
- What format should it be in?
- Who is this translation for (who is the end reader or end client)?

And remember, if you agree to something over the phone, always ask for written confirmation, or a payment order.

My Strategy

So, what do I recommend? I was once told to concentrate on two factors out of these four:

1. Be on time.
2. Do great work.
3. Charge a fair price.
4. Be somebody clients enjoy working with.

This might be a good tactic, but to me it seemed that if everyone else was concentrating on two or

112

even three of these factors, then I could get a leg up by featuring all four. I saw no reason not to, so that's what I do. The only thing that has changed over time was that I was able to be more picky about which clients to work with. In doing so, I raised the price I could charge, which also meant I got to start choosing more agreeable clients, which made me more agreeable with them. I have never wavered, on the other hand, from doing the best work I can do and being on time.

So, I know what you're thinking now: *"OK Rob, we know you're such an awesome, handsome and perfect[7] translator who can concentrate on all these points at once. But what if you're between a rock and a hard place for any reason?"*

Well, fine. If push really comes to shove, I would say the one point you absolutely positively never ever want to waver from is point number two - doing perfect work. The reason for this is that even if you are late, you charge too much, and are a pain to work with, clients often give you the benefit of the doubt if you do a really outstanding job.

---

[7] *(meek attempt at humorous sarcasm)*

The translation world is small and an agency may hear about you from another agency you worked for years ago. Maybe that previous agency client kept pushing you for a tight deadline. Or maybe you sent them something, but spotted a mistake later and you sent an improved copy with corrections ten minutes later. You might end up being too late and the client might have already sent your translation to their boss who in turn had already forwarded it to the board of directors, so your rapid response will be greatly appreciated by the client.

Say you got the change to them in time and they used your new copy for that job. So everything is fine, right? But the old copy you sent is still somewhere on their hard drive or in their email, and you never know whom they might send it to or when it could pop up again. For example, prospective client B may ask previous client A about your work, so previous client A will quickly look up your name and forward prospective client B the first example that pops up. So suddenly the prospective client B has a sub-par example of your work.

This may seem far-fetched, but after working in the industry for a while you'll start to see how intertwined these agencies can be and how people can switch jobs among them quite easily and quite often. So, while I'm sure you're an awesome translator, double-check and triple-check your work before sending it out.

Finding End Clients

Even though I keep saying you should leave these to later and that you should start with targeting agencies (or specific jobs that are posted on the main websites), I wanted to include at least a bit of information for finding end clients. As mentioned before, end clients are usually the companies that hire agencies. There are a few things to keep in mind:

- **End clients will often want translations in more than one language.** This may mean that you need to find other translators to work with, or just offer to handle one language and hope they accept that.

- **You will have to speak their language.** Here I don't mean "English" or "French", but I'm referring to the language of their industry. So, if they are in the finance world, they might be used to talking about P/E ratios and getting things completed this quarter and before tax season. You'll need to be able to relate to all this as well as ensure you don't slip into _"translator language"_, as they simply won't know what "source language" or "TEP" mean.

116

- **You will have to hold their hand.** They also won't know what timeline to ask for, what standard prices are, and what can be expected from a translator. You will have to be their guide throughout this process, and preferably without sounding too condescending. At the same time, you will need to make sure that the end result is really what they will need for business. If they ask you for something in traditional Chinese, but their client is in Shanghai, you might want to double-check that they've requested the correct translation!

- **You can concentrate more on your specialization.** If your specialization is food and beverage, then you may or may not receive that many requests on standard job sites. However, if you concentrate on end clients in the food & beverage and/or hospitality industry, chances are that all of your translations will be in your industry, which also means that you will be much more comfortable with all of the material.

- **You can get paid more.** And last, but definitely not least, end clients tend to pay more. Since they rely on you to perform all that work, they usually pay more than agencies. So if you can win a job from an end client, you will normally be able to ask for a higher rate.

So here goes:

Some Places to Find Potential End Clients

When searching for potential end clients, your best place to start off with is an online search. But of course, you can't just search for *"end client"*, so my advice is to start with the strategies outlined here below.

You will most likely be searching for companies that deal with an international aspect, since they will be requiring more than one language. So check out the **international chambers of commerce**. For example, if you are in Switzerland, check out the American chamber of commerce, the French Chamber of commerce, or equivalent for whichever language you work in.

You can also look up **international organizations** in your area. Consider also non-profits and educational groups which can help you secure excellent ratings in the beginning, even though they might not have the big budgets of companies to pay you a lot.

Don't forget to **join associations and groups** that deal with your specialization as well. So, if you specialize in legal translations, join your local legal associations and groups. Chances are, when you go to these meetings, you might be the only translator there. In fact, you may be the only non-lawyer there. And guess what? This is a great way to stand out and to be remembered.

You can also **attend fairs and events** in your specialty. If you don't want to join your local legal association (or maybe you can't, or it costs too much), then see if you can attend any events that lawyers attend in your area. This can also be a great opportunity to meet potential clients.

Is There a Potential Client You Would Love to Work For?

Have you considered any potential clients you admire for their work and you'd simply love to translate their material, or to be their regular translator? In that case, it is a good idea to show them that you are serious about working for them, and showing them that you prefer them over other companies.

First of all, why are you so interested in working for them? Is it because you have something in common with them? Are they in an industry you love? Do they have something to do with a passion of yours? In that case, let them know! Chances are they would love to have someone passionate working for them. Let them know you are available, and start off with the information about yourself as it applies to the company.

Offer to pass by for a coffee, or call them up directly. If you can meet them face to face it will give you a chance to explain why you are interested in their company and to show them that you are serious about it. Remember also to follow up with a handwritten note!

You can also offer to perform a translation for them for free. For example, let's say a restaurant you know has many clients that speak English, but it doesn't have a website or menus in English. You could simply translate their homepage for them, send it to them, and ask them if they'd like you to translate the rest while providing the homepage translation as a free gift. This also shows them that you are actually able to accomplish the job.

- Before Getting Started

- Let's Take a Step Back with Some Theory

- Starting Strategy

- Finding Clients

- **Marketing**

- Good Problems: You've Won an Assignment. Now What?

- Getting Paid

- Other Tips and Tricks to Keep In Mind

- Next Steps

HOW TO PROMOTE AND SELL YOUR TRANSLATION SERVICES, BOTH ONLINE AND OFF

Marketing

Finding a Job As a Freelancer

Before discussing marketing, it might be useful to go over expectations here. When you were in school, chances are you were taught how to find a job and you possibly then even found a job working for some company. So the drill you learned was:

Get into job searching mode → Find a job → Get out of job searching mode

Unfortunately, this approach doesn't work for freelance jobs. Once you find a good client/job, you can celebrate, then complete the job. But then you'll be searching for another client/job right away. In a certain sense, this never really stops, so you will always be in job searching mode. Of course, after a while you will have regular clients and so you can afford to be MUCH more selective about who to work with. However, marketing will constantly be in the back of your mind.

Keep this in mind while setting up your marketing campaigns. It is great to try new methods, but the methods that are sustainable

124

over a long period of time will likely be the best. Remember, freelancing is great, since it allows us the liberty to work on what we wish, where we wish, with the clients of our choosing, but in order to get there we are going to have to earn it!

I have divided this chapter into two sections: the first is Active Marketing, or marketing activities you must continue to do. These activities may change over time, but they will always be activities. The second is Passive Marketing, or marketing activities you need to set up once and then have work for you. It is probably best not to rely too much on the Passive Marketing activities, but you shouldn't neglect them either, since once they are set up they constitute little or no work, and you never know what new client you may reach as a result.

One thing to keep in mind throughout this whole, process, however, is that **your goal is to find new clients**. This may seem obvious, but you can lose track of your goal when you're designing marketing materials or maintaining a blog. I've known people whose blogs morphed into a travel blog, because they (rightly) thought travel videos would bring more views. The view count increased, but not the number of clients, due to the simple fact that most viewers weren't potential clients in need of translations.

Active Marketing

Personal Contacts

Your first type of marketing should be toward the "2 F's", or "Friends and Family". Presumably, you will have told them about your new career as a translation professional. If not, let them all know. Most people are more than happy to help out, and you never know who, among them, needs a translation or knows of someone who does. Remember, you can always offer a commission too for jobs they send your way.

Business Contacts

Next, you should turn to your business contacts. If your career thus far has had to do with translations, then this shouldn't be too hard at all. If, however, you work in any other industry, it is still worth a shot. Remember, it might sound intimidating, but you have nothing to lose and very much to gain. You can just send an email to past colleagues, clients, associates and contacts, and just let them know you are embarking on a career as a translation professional and to keep you in mind for future translation jobs.

If you are a student, or otherwise have no past colleagues, clients or associates, chances are you still have business contacts. Being a translator means you deal with various languages, and you've probably encountered plenty of people in both languages who aren't friends or family. These can all be potential clients. In fact, you might have already performed translations or interpretations as a favor in the past. These people already know of your abilities, so why not approach them as well?

Organizations

Join organizations in your area. Remember to not only join translation and language-related organizations, but organizations related to your specialties as well. If you specialize in financial translations, then find all the financial organizations in your area and join them. You might be the only translator in a room full of financiers, but what better way to stand out? The next time they need any translations done, they will remember you. You can obviously join as many organizations as you like, but try to stay active in the ones pertaining to translation and to your specialties. This means attending at least once a month or so.

Events

Look for upcoming events. Once again, these can deal with translations and languages, or with your specializations. If you specialize in legal translations, for example, find events held for lawyers, bar associations, etc., as well as events for legal researchers, law schools and law school alumni, and any other type of event relating to the legal field.

Google

Remember, you can find almost any client via a Google search or another search engine of your choice, such as Bing. Your first step should be translation agencies, but don't be afraid to contact end clients either. So, if you are good at translating websites, why not search for "Web Developers" in your metro area? Or any other types of businesses that may need translations? This means businesses that can either expand internationally, or that might cater to tourists or foreign nationals. Obviously, these will be cold contacts, so avoid sending a group email to a bunch of them. Instead, take the time to read about their business and to find the right person to contact within their organization.

Online Forums

You can find plenty of these on websites such as ProZ.com and Translatorscafe.com, but also on certain blogs, Facebook groups, Yahoo groups, etc. People often post questions regarding translation issues, so feel free to answer these as well as join general discussions that may be going on. These can bring you new contacts in the translation world, as well as provide valuable sources of information. And don't forget to find forums relating to your specializations as well, even if they have nothing to do with translation per se.

Your Blog

Maintaining a blog is a great way to create an online presence and new contacts, but is also one of the most time consuming. The basic litmus test for this is if you want to write stuff. Being a translator, chances are you feel comfortable writing, and if you like updating people on your progress, your life, what you learn, or anything else, then by all means, set up a blog. If, however, writing each post seems like a drag, and finding topics to write about seems daunting, then maybe this isn't for you.

You can set up a blog on a personal website, if you like, or on many free websites, such as Wordpress.com, Blogspot or Tumblr. Feel free to write up a few posts and experiment with your preferred style. Should you include photos? Should you write long posts or short posts? Should they be colloquial or more formal? Once you have some material, however, you should start searching for other blogs that are similar to yours. Here you can comment on their posts (possibly adding to what they wrote, or answering questions). Usually these blogs allow you to link back to your blog in your profile. You can also approach the blog owner to write a guest post for them and allow them to reciprocate if they wish.

Remember

And remember, now you have to rinse and repeat. Once again, you aren't doing all this marketing for a salaried job. When searching for a freelance job, you're searching for individual jobs, for individual clients, for regular clients, and everything in between. And while it does get easier and simpler over time, it never really goes away.

For this reason, I have divided up the marketing. Everything covered up to this point will have to be repeated regularly, so you may want to set a schedule. Of course, everything that follows is stuff that you can "set and forget". It will probably be worth checking up on those things from time to time as well, but they will be easier to maintain over time.

Passive Marketing

The following are "Passive Marketing" strategies, or strategies that, once set up, can be left alone while still reaping benefits. Obviously, many of them, such as a personal website, or LinkedIn, can also be active if you wish, but the sites listed below can all be passive if you like, and if you prefer to concentrate your efforts on other marketing endeavors.

Be Online

This ties back to having your own website (from the Pre-game chapter). An online presence is pretty much essential for people to find you. This can be via your personal website or blog, a ready-made site such as About.me, LinkedIn, or even your profile page on ProZ.com, etc. Remember that each one has pros and cons. If you have your own website, you can personalize is at much as you like, and even maintain a blog if you wish, along with a resume, past clients, or anything else you'd like. Then again, it will likely come to cost around $1,000 or so, after domain name registration, web hosting, hiring a website designer and coder, and having someone available for periodic updates or fixing bugs. Also, it is much harder to find your website via a search engine than it is to find an established website like ProZ.com. This is due to Search Engine Optimization, or SEO, which websites like ProZ.com and LinkedIn have a lot of experience with. These can be personalized to a certain extent, but they are free, easy to update, and have a certain amount of SEO built into them already.

E-mail Signature

This is an easy addition that can help out as well. Most email programs allow you to add an email signature, or a few lines below each outgoing email. The best option here is to make it a few lines at most. Anything else is overkill and might seem like an advertisement. For example, mine says:

—

Robert Gebhardt

www.LuganoTranslations.com - *Bringing the World Closer Together, One Translation at a Time*

Along these lines, you can also personalize other things, like your status on Skype or Google chat, or your tagline on forums and meetup groups.

LinkedIn

This is the main social network for professionals, and you should definitely join it. For the setup, you can refer to the Pre-game chapter, since the format follows pretty much the same format as all other professional websites. Once you are done you should add your website (if you have one) and links to your ProZ.com account and any other accounts you might have.

Once your profile is complete, you can search for organizations and groups to join (See Organizations, under Marketing – Active) above. Obviously, you can be very active via LinkedIn if you wish, and over time you will get a better idea as to what works for you, but for now, you should make sure you at least have an updated and searchable profile.

Facebook

Chances are, you already have a Facebook account. The important thing here is to have a plan ahead of time. Since Facebook tends to be for personal use, decide ahead of time how many work-related posts you want to be sending to your friends and how often. Obviously, some of them will be good, and you'll want to keep your friends updated and be able to use them as possible contacts. But you also don't want to annoy them with daily sales tactics or to harass them for more business.

Here's what works for me. I simply created a friends list called "Professional" made up of business contacts, and every now and then I send out posts and links only to these contacts. For the most part, however, I save Facebook posts for major news.

Twitter

Twitter is similar to Facebook in that it is a social network, but many things are different as well. First of all, although Twitter doubled the character limit from 140 to 280 characters for each post, you should still try to keep things short and sweet, especially when you're including links and images as well. Secondly, you don't have to follow people back in order for them to follow you. In fact, they don't have to follow you at all in order to see your posts, and likewise, you can see everyone else's posts (unless they make them private). Of course, if you follow people you are guaranteed to receive their posts. Anyway, it is worth setting up a Twitter account as well. In fact, you can then search Twitter using something like "looking for translators" and see if anyone is looking for a translation to be done. You never know!

Connecting Accounts

This is especially valid if you have a blog or if you use any type of social media. The idea is that, any time you write a new blog post, you automatically send out a Facebook message, Tweet and/or LinkedIn message with a link to the blog post. However, if you don't have a blog, you can also set it up so every new Facebook message (or every Facebook message with a certain hashtag) creates a new Tweet and/or LinkedIn message, among many other things. The best source for this is IFTTT.com (IFTTT stands for "If This Then That"). You can connect your accounts and set it up so, if something happens in one account, something else should happen in another account. It can all be personalized as much as you like as well, so check it out at www.IFTTT.com.

Stickers / Postcards

Remember that all the other translators looking for jobs will have a resume and, possibly, business cards. So why not include stickers or postcards with your name or logo? This can make you more memorable and help you to stand out from the crowd. Then again, these should be in addition to normal business cards rather than as a substitute, since no one wants to put a sticker or postcard in their wallet or Rolodex. Other ideas could be pens or notebooks, so that potential clients will be constantly reminded of you whenever they use them.

If design is not your strong suit, find someone to design a sticker or postcard, since it takes a bit more skill than a normal business card. You can always ask a friend for a favor, or, worst-case scenario, feel free to check out Fiverr.com (design jobs can be done for $5 here), or 99designs.com (where designers compete for your business, and you only pay for what you choose to use). Canva is also a great site and offers ready-made templates.

- Before Getting Started

- Let's Take a Step Back with Some Theory

- Starting Strategy

- Finding Clients

- Marketing

•Good Problems: You've Won an Assignment. Now What?

- Getting Paid

- Other Tips and Tricks to Keep in Mind

- Next Steps

REFER TO THIS SECTION ONCE YOU'VE BEEN HIRED FOR YOUR FIRST JOB

Good Problems: You've Won an Assignment. Now What?

I realize that so far I've been giving you quite a bit of work. Obviously, if this process were any simpler, many more people would be doing it. The truth is that many try, but relatively few succeed, and this is testament to the fact that it pays to do things the right way. The good thing about this process is that there are a certain number of steps that, if followed correctly, help you out immensely. So, while many of these steps may seem tedious or redundant, they will certainly bring rewards in the long term.

Now, however, we get to talk about how to deal with the good problems (no, not what to do with all the money you earn. That one's on you). The first one is going through a checklist.

A Checklist

Let's assume you've been assigned a job. You should probably keep this checklist handy before confirming that you're going ahead just to make sure:

- **Do you know your rate?** Has your rate been clearly stated and accepted?
- **Do you know the deadline?** Is it clear to both parties?
- **Have you seen the actual file to be translated in full?** You don't want any surprises after you've already accepted the job.
- **Do you know what format they want the translation in?** Usually, it will be either MS Word or the same format sent to you, but you never know.

And some optional points:

- **Who is the audience?** Are you absolutely clear on who the audience is? Writing text for children or adults can be very different. Or is this being used for marketing purposes?
- **Do they have a glossary of terms?** If they have performed similar translations (of manuals, products, etc.) in the past, they might have a glossary of terms they prefer to use.

This may seem like quite a few questions to bother the client with, especially someone who isn't quite yet a client and you probably don't want to bother with too many questions. So how can you make sure you have all this information without completely annoying the other person? I find the best way is to send a simple email saying something along the lines of:

Hello,

Thank you for your email. I hereby confirm that I will translate XYZ file, which I have seen, for a total price of XXX. I will deliver it by YYY at Y:00 o'clock. I can deliver it in MS Word format.

Please let me know if this is acceptable to you, and I would appreciate it if you could let me know if you have any other pertinent information (like a glossary, information on the target audience, etc.)

Thank you very much![8]

---

[8] See "5 Things You Can Add to Your Terms of Service" in the "Tips and Tricks" section for some other things you can add to your terms of service.

Tracking Jobs

Now let's assume the client confirmed all the above information and you're excited to get started. Go ahead and do your best! Chances are that right after being assigned a new job, you're revving to make a dent in it. So by all means give it your absolute best shot. Before you close up for the night, however, (and certainly before you deliver the job to the client), you should take care of one more thing. **You should collect as much information as you can about this client**.

This includes the name of whoever emailed you, the link to the job announcement URL, if available, as well as any email addresses, physical addresses, websites, etc. Remember to collect phone numbers, as well as any other email addresses there may be for the same company. Physical addresses and phone numbers are best, since they make the client accessible offline as well. Also, don't be shy about asking for their information. If the client is legitimate, there should be no issue in providing whatever information you need.

This information will be used later for invoicing (See the "Getting Paid" chapter), but will also come in handy if the client starts delaying or postponing the payment date or, even worse, becomes incommunicado.

These are the steps I take when I am assigned a new task:

1. Open my Google spreadsheet and enter:
   a. Job number (chronological)
   b. Client's name
   c. Client's contact details (emails, physical address, instant messenger, phone number, Skype, etc. Namely, everything you can capture)
   d. Name of job (usually just the name of the document to be translated)
   e. Number of words
   f. Rate per word
   g. Total amount due
   h. Date payment is due
2. Perform the translation
3. At the end of the week, check whether the client needs an invoice
4. If so, generate an invoice with the client and job details filled out (we'll cover more about invoices in the chapter "Getting Paid").

Now, this may seem like quite a bit of work, but you get used to it over time. Especially when you have a monthly total and you're happy with every addition to the total sum.

The main point here is that you want to make invoicing as easy as possible. Otherwise, you may find yourself delaying the invoicing process, which is unwise. Never forget you're doing this to provide yourself with a better life (as in, making money to live that life), not to provide the world with better-translated documents (although you end up providing that as a nice bonus).

Take the time at the end of the day to collect all the information you can, as well as tally up the total amount you will be earning, which is always a satisfying exercise.

Dealing with Translation Challenges

Things can always pop up. Maybe some part of the document isn't clear, there are some mistakes in the source text, or you realize that you simply cannot finish by the deadline, or you're not sure about certain instructions.

Whatever pops up, the best way is always to **contact the client right away**. It doesn't matter whether it's the client's fault or yours. Even if you don't think you can make the deadline, it is much better to let the client know a few days ahead of time than to wait until the deadline has passed. This might seem obvious when reading it, but in the midst of a situation, it might feel natural to take longer and hope the client doesn't notice that you are late, or something along those lines. I seriously advise against this. If the deadline isn't fixed, then the client actually won't care too much and will appreciate your candor. If it is a fixed deadline, letting the client know ahead of time will give them the chance to handle it, either by extending the deadline, or possibly finding another translator to help you out, etc.

Having said that, **you do not want to contact the client for 'every single thing'**. If an issue pops up that is not too urgent, then it might be best to wait

146

before contacting the client, just in case something else pops up. This is because it is much better to consolidate everything in one email rather than send many different emails and keep bothering the client. For example, if part of the document is unclear, you can wait to see if there are any other parts of the document that are unclear before emailing the client. If the deadline isn't imminent, maybe wait until the end of the day in case you come across another issue. It's always best to group things up and send just one email to the client, with a few bullet points showing the issues you found.

Dealing with Mistakes in the Source Text

Every now and then you will find mistakes in the source text. Handling them will always be a judgment call, but in short, these are your choices:

1. Correct the mistake.
2. Ignore the mistake.
3. Ask the client.

If you choose 1 or 2, you can also add a note to the translation to detail what you decided and why. Usually the choice is somewhat obvious, although I like adding the note just to make sure sometimes. If it isn't obvious, then feel free to ask the client, possibly detailing each option.

147

You also have the option of writing [sic] next to the text, but this is rarely used in translations.

Other Translation Factors to Keep in Mind

I know you already have enough on your plate, but I thought I would add these points just to keep in the back of your mind while working on the translation. As long you read through this once it should stick with you:

- Be reachable. Check your email regularly in case the client has an update.
- Don't bother your client too much with every little issue (mentioned above).
- Re-check the client's instructions before sending out the translation.
- Don't get into fights with the client, even if they are wrong. It isn't worth it. Just move on.

- Before Getting Started

- Let's Take a Step Back with Some Theory

- Starting Strategy

- Finding Clients

- Marketing

- Good Problems: You've Won an Assignment. Now What?

• Getting Paid

- Other Tips and Tricks to Keep in Mind

- Next Steps

HOW TO ENSURE YOU ARE PAID / HOW TO ASK FOR MONEY / HOW TO ACCEPT PAYMENT

Getting Paid

Now you've won your translation job, you're getting the hang of things and you're doing just great. That's awesome. It really is. But remember that the goal of this whole process is to provide you with a paycheck. So, while you're doing your job well, you need to make sure you get paid for doing it.

Translation providers are NOTORIOUSLY bad at paying. I really cannot emphasize this enough. Most of them are honest and even good people. But for some reason, translation agencies seem to think that most market rules don't apply to them. For an example, check out the video *"The Vendor Client relationship in real world situations"* here: http://www.youtube.com/watch?v=RCheZyb2qxU. Seriously, ask translators who have been at it for a number of years and get ready for some odd stories.

As a brief example, I was once hired by an agency for a translation at a certain price. I delivered on time and the agency was happy. Later that week, however, the agency sent an email saying, *"The end client was happy with the translation, so we'd like to make them even more happy and offer a discount. So how about cutting 10% from your prices so we can make them happier for future jobs?"* Yeah, seriously.

More common, however, is to have payday come and go, emails asking for payment ignored, and finally, when you do get an answer, get a reply that says (typos and bad grammar are not mine):

>>i can pay you as soon the customer pay me. He tells me february.
sorty<<

In case you were wondering, this is the exact reply I received from a client after my fifth email asking why payment was late. This is the amount of explanation I had to go with. And this client had even added me on Facebook and given me her phone number!

So, before you run off back to the nine to five world, let me set your mind at ease. While clients do come up with ridiculous excuses, practices, and stories, you can certainly resolve these with a steadfast demeanor, making sure your behind is covered at the same time.

Escrow Services

The first and main point here is to use an escrow service if at all possible. If you're using websites like Upwork.com, then you have to use their escrow service, which is great. Some websites offer optional escrow services, which you should always opt for. These sites take a percentage commission when you use these services, but trust me, they're worth it, if for nothing else than peace of mind.

In case you're unsure about the process, this is how an escrow service works: the client pays the full amount in advance to a third party, usually either a bank or a financial branch of a company. Once the transaction has taken place and the escrow account is funded, you'll usually receive a notification. This notification will also show a deadline, after which the money is sent to you. This deadline should coincide more or less with the due date of the job. At this point, you can start working and deliver the job to the client. Once you have delivered the work, the funds in the escrow account are released and sent to you.

Obviously, if there is a problem with the work, the client may opt to block the release of funds, but this doesn't mean the client gets the money back. This only means the client would have to give an explanation (and so would you). The escrow company then decides how to proceed. While this can be an issue, I have never encountered this problem, so I won't go into any further detail about it.

Other points to keep in mind:

1. Collect as much information about the client as you can.
2. Ask for partial payments.
3. Password protect your completed files.
4. Look out for red flags.

Collect as Much Information as You Can

If you followed the steps listed under the *"Good Problems"* chapter then this step should already be completed. If not, please check the *"Tracking Jobs"* section of that chapter.

Ask for Partial Payments

For new clients, and especially for big jobs, feel free to ask for a partial payment. This payment can even be a small percentage, but the willingness to pay shows a great deal. Most payment methods give you an immediate notification. If they don't you can still ask for proof of payment from the client. These should be enough to start your job. I know these could technically be forged, but I have yet to hear of a client who went that far.

Password Protect Your Files

Remember this isn't foolproof, so you may end up just annoying an honest provider, while merely inconveniencing someone who is trying to cheat you. In fact, you can find programs and tutorials on YouTube teaching you how to hack into a password-protected file. However, chances are most people don't know how to do it. If you're afraid you're dealing with a slacker client who might get a bit too lazy and never send a payment over, a password-protected file could be the kick they need to realize they'd better hurry up.

Look out for Red Flags

The first red flag is a non-company email address (such as a Yahoo or Gmail address). If a company is contacting you, they'd better have a damn good reason for not using their company email address. However, private individuals may contact you at any point, so don't discount Yahoo or Gmail correspondence straight away. If, however, they only have a web-based address, it is probably wise to ask for references, partial payment up-front, or at least a phone number.

Invoices

If you have 10 different clients, you will have 10 different requirements for invoices. ProZ and other sites offer their own invoices, but unless you can make a payment through the website itself, as is the case with Upwork and Twago, chances are you will have to issue your own invoice.

I have found that the best way to issue invoices is once per week. Don't wait until the end of the month, since most payment terms start from the invoice date and not the translation delivery date. The invoice writing process starts when you are assigned the task.

Here is a copy of my invoice template:

INVOICE 405

Date of Issue: February 27th, 2015

Bill From: Acahi
www.Acahi.com
5390 Peachtree Industrial Blvd.
Atlanta, GA 30305
USA

Bill To: John Client
Client Company Ltd.
John@ClientCompany.eu
www.ClientCompany.eu
VAT: 0987654321

TOTAL DUE	
€	789.76

FOR:

Description	Rate		# of words		Line Total	
Contract 045 (EN-ZH)	€	0.08	7372		€	589.76
website translation					€	200.00
					€	-
				Total:	€	789.76

Date Due: March 6th, 2015   (7 days from issue)
Payable via Paypal or Bank transfer (Paypal email: Info@Acahi.com)

Invoices more than 30 days overdue are subject to a 10% late fee.

Happy with my service? Please refer me! You will receive a 5% discount per file for every
successful referral!

Here, you can ignore the logo at the top (I
added it when I decided to get incorporated, which I

will discuss later). All the other information is taken from my spreadsheet (from the *Tracking Jobs* section of the *Good Problems to Have* chapter).

Then, all I do is click Print and choose the option *"Save as PDF"*. This gives me a nice PDF file without the row and column lines that I can send to the client.

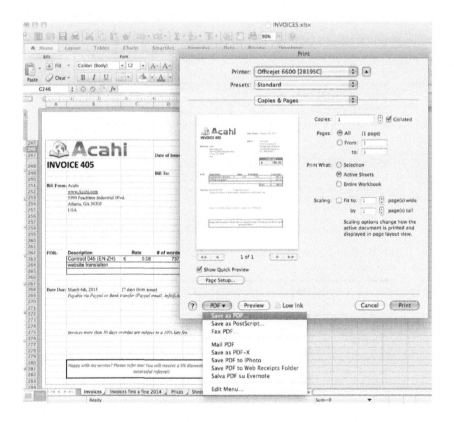

Also, if you're just starting out and you feel a bit insecure about using the number INVOICE 001, feel free to start wherever you want. These invoice numbers are for you, so you can start with INVOICE 101 or any other number, as long as you continue them in chronological order.

The information next to "Bill From" never changes, since it is mine, while the information next to "Bill To" remains the same for each client.

Next to "FOR", I copy the information my Google spreadsheet ("Tracking jobs", under "Good Problems: You've won an assignment, now what?"). If the client uses any reference number, you should include that here as well. Feel free to show a rate and wordcount if you feel it's appropriate. The important point is the money due, so triple-check those numbers, and include the amount.

Note how I have placed that big green box in a very prominent place so that the client has no reason to question which number is the amount due. Obviously, the client is going through many different invoices too, so showing this number very clearly helps them out and means you don't risk their misreading something and paying you an incorrect amount.

As you can see at the bottom, I have a due date that is net 7 days from issue. Usually a client will specify their due date, for example, 7 days, 15 days or 30 days. If they don't, however, I usually write, *"Payable upon receipt,"* so that it is due right away, or *"7 days"*, which gives a precise due date. If the client wants to pay you 60 or 90 days after the invoice (or anything that is too long for you), try to negotiate something quicker if possible, or at least a partial payment to show good faith.

Lastly, you may have noticed the advertisement in red at the bottom. I didn't have this at the beginning, but as time goes by and you become more comfortable with what you do, you will appreciate your invoice as another marketing mechanism. For example, next to your name or slogan you can have something similar to what I wrote, or even something cheesy like, *"Receive a hat with my company/country/whatever logo on it for ordering at least ten jobs from me"*. An invoice can be seen as valuable real estate. So why not use every part of it, rather than just leave empty space? This obviously doesn't mean you should clutter it up as much as possible, but a sentence or two in the right place could go a long way, and it certainly won't hurt!

Other Additions You Can Make To Your Invoice

Although I don't include them in mine, there are various additions you can make to your invoices should you wish:

A deadline for reworking. Every now and then, the client may ask you to rework or modify a translation you've made. For the most part, it is wise to do so to keep the client happy, since it implies you've made a mistake. However, you also want to make sure the client doesn't contact you five months later and ask you to rework a translation you forgot all about as part of the same invoice. The way to do this is to set a deadline. Something along the lines of *"All rewrites and edits shall be made within 30 days, after which no claims will be considered"* would work well for this.

Retaining copyright. Sometimes, you might not get paid your full amount or might not get paid at all. And while you are chasing the client for your money, the client is already using your translation on their documents or website. You can protect yourself against this by writing something along the lines of *"translator retains copyright of this work until invoice is paid in full"*. This way you can pursue them for copyright violation.

161

Opportunity to redeem yourself. Occasionally the client may find a few mistakes in your translation and use that as a reason to pay you less. Sometimes they may be entitled to do so. However, you might want to give yourself the chance to redeem yourself, so if they find something wrong with your translation, you can then work on it for them again before they decide to lower the price.

Fun with Invoices

You can actually do much more with your invoices besides a request for a referral if you wish. For example, if you are already donating to charity, why not say something like *"five percent of what you pay will be donated to XYZ charity,"* or to the victims of a natural disaster, or anything else you hold dear? Chances are, if you hold it dear, others do as well, so a message like that could put you and your client in the same boat, so to speak.

You could also list any awards you have won recently (why not?), or newly acquired skills, in case your clients aren't up to date.

Another idea is a little something to make the client smile, like a small drawing or an amusing quote that changes from invoice to invoice.

Invoices are quite dreary, and for a client they are a reminder of a payment (when was the last time you were happy to see a utility or a phone bill?). So sprucing it up a bit can always be a nice touch.

How to Collect Your Money Once It's Due

Now, once again, the good thing about gaining more experience working with different clients is you can choose to go with those clients who pay you on time rather than those who don't. In the meantime, you will have to start implementing a collection method. And remember, no matter how angry or frustrated you may be, the client still has your money, so wait to vent your anger until **after** you receive it.

If you have not received your payment by the due date listed on your spreadsheet, send a polite email to your client reminding them that the payment is due and asking when you can expect payment. At this point, I automatically set a reminder on Google calendar for two days later than the due date. If you still have no response, send a second email, asking when you can expect your payment due, and set reminders for every other day from that point on.

At this stage, you are trying to be so persistent that the client has to deal with you. In 90% of the cases, you will receive a reply within one week giving you a more definite payment date, or you will receive the payment itself.

If, after one week, I don't hear from the client, I send an email to every other email address I can find from the client's company. This includes using info@... and contact@... . This way, I can be sure that the client's colleagues (and boss) know that he is late with his payment. The tone of my email is always very polite.

If I still receive no reply, I try one final email and wait another two days. At this point, if the client is still incommunicado, I use their phone number to call them. I often say I am calling on behalf of Robert. I confess I don't know if this is a better tactic, but it seems if they think a whole organization is behind me, they might be more likely to take me seriously. In addition, I also contact the website through which they contacted me, like ProZ.com, to tell them that I have not heard from the client at all.

How Not To Get Screwed Over By A Client (Part II)

After you start freelancing, you'll notice a clear and wide discrepancy between your deadlines and your client's deadlines. If your deadline is Friday at noon, you will start getting emails at Friday around 11:30 a.m. at the latest. Chances are you will need to send progress reports (what you have done so far) once a day leading up to Friday. If, however, your payment is due next Friday, you can expect to not hear from the client all day. When you finally email them, you can expect a reply on Monday or Tuesday, asking for another invoice from you, because they need you to mention their VAT number and your physical address (or something else) on their invoice. So, you will send it right away, and then you can expect more silence. You then send another follow up on Wednesday, asking for confirmation that they received the new invoice, and asking can you expect payment. They will reply Thursday, saying that it will take another 30 days now, since the new invoice just came in. This means that 30 days later you will be chasing them again, only this time their accountant isn't there until Monday.

This might be a slight exaggeration, but I kept track of payment delivery times for one month (I only did it for this one month, so I can't say if it was indicative, although it seemed like an average month to me at the time). This particular month's payment arrived with an average delay of more than a week.

Now things are better, since I've been able to be pickier about clients.

My last resort is to pay a personal visit to the client. This obviously has geographical restrictions (and I'm assuming you got into this business because you don't like those). But you may have family or good friends close to the client. At this point, depending on the total amount due, it may be worth offering half of the payment to whoever can pass by the client with a copy of your invoice and insist upon payment. I have only reached this stage once, so when my friend called to say she was passing by to collect my money later that day (and called from a local number) they sent their payment right away.

I always wait to write a review on the Blue Board until after I receive payment. Once again, this is because I want to remain outwardly polite while the client is still holding my money. If, however, you don't even hear from the client after a month, even if you receive full payment with an apology after that, you should probably write them up on the Blue Board. Chances are you don't want to work for them again, and you should warn fellow freelancers about them as well.

Charging Interest

Can you start charging interest once payment is due? Well, this might actually depend on your country of residence. For example, most of Europe will allow you to charge interest as long as certain rules such as prompt notification are being followed. So look into what laws apply for your own country. You also, however, have to keep in mind that your client might or might not want to deal with interest. I have found that the more you take your own payment seriously, the more the client will take it seriously. If you can seriously charge interest and are able to do it correctly, then by all means do so. Just keep in mind to have it clearly stated on your invoice, and also realize that some clients may not take it as seriously. This may be a good litmus test as to which clients you want to keep working with in the future.

What to Do When Not Receiving Payment - My Personal Example

Here is an example of what happened to me with a client who ended up disappearing. Hopefully you can learn from my mistakes and see what I did right and what I did wrong. Initially, I received an alert from Translatorsbase that there was a new job matching my credentials, so when I opened the notification this was what I saw:

translatorsbase.com

IT translation

I would like to get a document in Italian translated into English. There are about 5,000 words.

I need the translated document by 13th January, morning UK time

Status :	Closed
Project ID :	130704
Project Type :	None
Source Language :	Italian
Target Language :	English
Date Created :	01/09/2013
Due Date :	01/13/2013
Country :	Not Defined
Area of expertise :	Not Defined
Tools :	Not Defined
Work Areas :	Translation
Word Count :	5000
Delivery File Type :	Not Defined
Only certified translators :	No

Close

Translation Jobs | Translation Articles | Translation Forums

Websites for translators | Free Translation | Free Word Count Tool | Translation Rates

| Bookmark Us | Privacy Policy

www.translatorsbase.com

The client was someone I had never worked with previously called John Morgan. When I clicked on his profile, this is what I saw:

And here is my offer, with subsequent correspondence. As you can see, he sent me an online link where I could download the document. After some back and forth we agreed that I was to translate the final section.

Robert Gebhardt

Hello John Morgan,

I am an Italian-English translator and I would be happy to assist you with your 5,000 word translation.

I have published articles for Cornell University''s The Current, was a columnist for The International Affairs Journal and have been published in the Swiss-Italian paper Corriere del Ticino.

Moreover, having an Italian mother and an American father, and having grown up in both the United States and Italy, I am truly bilingual.

You can find more information, including some sample translations, on my Proz profile page here: http://www.proz.com/profile/1494149

I am ready to begin at your convenience. If you have any questions please feel free to let me know.

Thank you,

Robert
http://about.me/robertgebhardt

John Morgan

Thank you for your quote. Please find the files for translation here: https://app.box.com/s/68i51tuiwbu5uk6cq6jf There are about 25,000 words. How many words could you translate by Monday morning? Regards, John

Robert Gebhardt

Hello John, Thank you for your email. I should be able to complete around 5,000 words by Monday morning if that works for you. Thank you, Robert

John Morgan

Sorry for so late reply. You can download the word version from here: https://app.box.com/s/19yrcw0yaiakvwxhd6e4 If you could translate from the page 86 till the end(2,377 words), that would be great. Regards, John

Robert Gebhardt

That sounds good. Just as a confirmation, I will translate from page 86 according to the PDF file, or page 86/99, from the illustration starting with "SALA SERRA" until the end of the document. I imagine you would like the illustrations translated as well, correct? Thank you, Robert

John Morgan

Yes, please translate the illustrations as well. Thanks John

John Morgan

Hi Robert, How is it going with the translation so far? Regards, John

Robert Gebhardt

Hi John, It's going well so far. If any issues come up I will let you know, otherwise I should have it done by Monday morning (if not tomorrow night). Thank you, Robert

Robert Gebhardt

Hi John, I have finished the translation, but since I cannot add an attachment via this text box, could you please send me an email address you would like it sent to? Also, I see that you do not have a complete profile on translatorsbase, no feedback and you do not have a website. So I have password protected the document, until you can send me a partial payment of USD 100 (Paypal email: info@Acahi.com) and/or a website with your information. I apologize for the inconvenience, but I have been cheated by clients in the past, so the first time I do business with a new client I prefer to play it safe on principle. Thank you very much, Robert

John Morgan

You can send the file to: jomorgantrans@yahoo.co.uk I will try to pay today or tomorrow. Regards, John

Robert Gebhardt

Hello John, Could you please let me know when I can expect payment? Thank you, Robert

Robert Gebhardt

Hello John, It is now 10 days since I delivered the file. You owe me 237.70. Could you let me know when I can expect payment? Thank you, Robert

Robert Gebhardt

Hello John, Please let me know when I can expect payment. Thank you, Robert

After sending a number of messages to his email address I then contacted translatorsbase.com.

--Original Message--
Hello,

I had an issue with a client here. His name is John Morgan and this is the project url: http://translatorsbase.com/view_project.aspx?nav=mybids&project_id=130704&p=0&st=2

I completed job and sent the (password protected) translation to him, but I haven't heard back since. It seems obvious he figured out how to crack the password and has no intention of paying me, so I was just wondering if I have any recourse. In order to post a job on this website I imagine he had to pay something, or provide some personal information, correct?

Once again, the project ID is: 130704

And all the information I can gather from the site is:

Email : jomorgantrans@yahoo.co.uk
First Name :   John
Last Name :   Morgan
Address :   92 Middlesex Street
Zip :   E1 7EZ
City : London
Country :   United Kingdom

Thank you very much,

Robert

To which, their response was:

Hello,

Thank you for your email. Unfortunately, he is not responding to our emails.
We will ensure that this client will never post projects on our website again. We suspended this user due to violation of our policy and we will track this person's future activity on our site. We have informed him that he is not allowed to post projects on our website or to bid on projects.
Sorry, I could not be much help on this issue.

Best Regards,

Translatorsbase.com Support
****

Needless to say, the address and phone number were both bogus. The address exists, but it seems to be a residential address in London. So, let's analyze this. What did I do right?

1. I took down all the information I had available.
2. I requested further information before delivery.
3. I protected the file with a password.

And what did I do wrong?

1. I didn't request further company details such as a company website.
2. I didn't insist on pre-payment before delivery.
3. I relied on password protection.

What I'm trying to point out is that I did most things right but this was still avoidable. When you start a new job, you are worried about the job itself. I was concentrating on the terminology, on how to translate the illustrations and display them as in the original, etc. But I should not have forgotten that I am only doing all this to get paid. Because all the time and effort I spent working on that translation was wasted time and effort.

Some Other Examples Of Bad Excuses

Here are some other examples of excuses and reasons I've received for late or non-payment. Obviously by no means an exhaustive list:

"The bank is processing the payment." This is the modern equivalent of "the check's in the mail". Ensure you ask for proof of payment.

"The end client has not paid me yet." An agency I worked with continued saying this for two months, and when I finally offered to contact the end client on their behalf, they threatened me with legal action.

"You didn't send me the invoice." When you obviously have. Another version is "We need XYZ information added to the invoice".

"We will pay you after the next job." I honestly wonder if anyone accepts this as true.

"CLIENT'S NAME is in the hospital now." I actually got this one twice. In one case, saying the client was in the hospital for at least a week, unfortunately the client forgot she had added me on Facebook. Around one hour later she posted an invite to a party at her house in two days' time. The answer here is that business life still goes on, as callous as business life may be.

After You Get Paid

So, you've now found a client, won an assignment, completed it successfully, and you've been paid. At this stage, you're probably thinking: *"What? I'm not done yet?"* Well, technically, yes. But since you've gone through all that and successfully completed the job, why not try to get everything you can out of it. Especially when what you can get is a referral and/or rating.

Referrals and Ratings

Those of you who follow me on YouTube (*hint hint:* *https://www.youtube.com/c/freelancetranslatortips*), know how much I go on and on about this. I've also mentioned it a couple times in this book, but here I will give this topic its own section. The fact is, when you are first starting out, ratings and referrals are extremely important and can help you get future jobs. In fact, each new rating/referral will be a permanent help when searching for future clients.

My advice here is to have a platform in mind ahead of time. Usually this will be something like ProZ.com, Translatorscafe.com, or another similar website. For our purposes, let's assume you are using ProZ.com. This means that you plan on using

ProZ.com to find many, if not most, of your future clients. In this case, you want to build up your profile on this website as much as possible.

So how do you do this? Well, luckily ProZ.com makes it pretty simple. Once you have completed a translation (I usually recommend doing this right after payment), you can email the client, thanking them for payment and/or the opportunity, and then (nicely) ask them if they could leave you a good rating on your profile. ProZ.com makes it as easy as a simple click of a button:[9]

---

[9] You can find the actual page here:
https://www.proz.com/translator-feedback/request

Email message to be sent

From name:	
From email:	
Subject:	Please help me by giving feedback about my service

Customize your message below:

I've appreciated the opportunity to work together with you.

If you're satisfied with my service, please consider entering translator feedback for me at ProZ.com. Your doing so will help me build a strong profile, which is important to me in my service as an independent professional working for you and your company.

You can enter feedback by clicking one of the links at the bottom of this message.

Thank you in advance for your consideration. Whether or not you choose to enter feedback, I look forward to working with you again in the future.

Best regards,
YOUR NAME

This box will be automatically appended to your message:

Please take a moment to give feedback by simply clicking one of the links below.

- **Yes**, I'd be **willing to work again** with this service provider, to whom I've outsourced work before.

- I prefer to **not give feedback** to this service provider at this time.

Or, see more feedback choices.

Alternately, you can copy this URL into your web browser:
https://www.proz.com/translator-feedback/give-feedback/eid_s/1494149

As you can see, it also gives them other choices, such as being able to write up their own review or leave you a score, but in essence they can just get by with one click. This is as simple as it gets.

Be aware that any rating will remain on your profile forever and this will keep paying dividends over time. One successful job can add a new rating that you get to use throughout your career. Of course, this also means that you should only ask for ratings & reviews from clients who are satisfied with your work.

- Before Getting Started

- Let's Take a Step Back with Some Theory

- Starting Strategy

- Finding clients

- Marketing

- Good Problems: You've Won an Assignment. Now What?

- Getting Paid

•Other Tips and Tricks to Keep in Mind

- Next Steps

OTHER ISSUES YOU MAY COME ACROSS AND WAYS TO GET AHEAD IN THIS BUSINESS

Other Tips and Tricks to Keep in Mind

Optical Character Recognition (OCR)

Your personal methods for translations may vary, but chances are that at some point you've had to deal with a PDF file, a scanned document, a hard copy, an image, or any other form of document that did not contain text per se, but an image of the text. So how can you insert your text into your CAD program, or just into Word? If there are several thousand words, then rewriting everything in the original language just so you can rewrite it in the target language seems like a colossal waste of time.

Luckily, technology has come to the rescue and we have something called Optical Character Recognition (OCR). This recognizes characters and displays them as words onto a document for you. The quality will only be as good as the program, but the better the program the more it will cost.

---

[10] *Disclaimer: Once again, I am not getting any payment or any benefit of any sort to name names. It's just a program I like very much.*

At one point, I used one of the free options. I tried searching for it, but for the life of me I can't remember the name. Regardless, now I've switched to a paid one, which I recommend whenever people ask. It's called onlineocr.net[10]. The prices are quite cheap, at $17.95 for 300 pages at the time of writing. I just prepay for a few hundred and I know it will always be available. You can even choose the source language you are working from. I can't speak for other languages, but I have found it to be quite good for both Italian and English.

Time Management

As freelancers, entrepreneurs, and people who do not work for a boss, time management becomes critical. Any freelancer is familiar with the feeling *"Well, I could just watch TV right now. No one would notice."* or, even worse *"Well, I got into business for myself so I wouldn't have to deal with too much stress, why not relax right now?"*

Let's face it, when you have a boss, you just need to do what you are told. Even when you're not busy, you are spending time trying to look busy. What happens when all of that goes away? Can you really stay at home not doing anything? Well, of course not. And hopefully that's not why you got into business for yourself. The goal of anything you do should never be idleness. With the limited number of hours and days we get on this planet, it makes no sense to waste any more time than we have to.

I know I still have had quite a few issues with this. I would get burned out, take time off, panic because there was no business, jump back in and then work too hard again, repeat this process over and over. Because of this, I got very deep into **time management**. So, based on what I have learned, I will make some personal recommendations and give you some basic pointers. However, if this is a topic you really want to treat fairly, I'd recommend reading some good books about the topic. I even have an order in which I recommend them, which I will show you right after my recommendations below:

1. Embrace lists, labels and folders
Everything you have should be retrievable at a moment's notice. I actually try to have as little as I can in physical format as it helps when I'm traveling. And everything I do have is labeled clearly, especially on my computer where I treat everything like my cabinet and everything is easily retrievable. If need be, I take time out every month or so to make sure it is. And no, "*Miscellaneous*" and "*other*" are not labels.

2. Plan your day the day before

When you go to sleep, you should have the next day planned out. By all means, leave some time for surprises, but not too much. Your life isn't as exciting as you think it may be. I recommend planning your most important or hardest item as the first thing to do the next morning.

3. Do NOT check email first thing in the morning

You already have your most important task planned out. No matter who emailed you, they can wait until after you have completed that task. This can vary, but I recommend checking emails at set times during the day, ideally only 2 or 3 times. Remember, emails are a great way of keeping busy and making you feel like you're doing things without accomplishing anything. Inboxes are interruptions and to-do lists that other people have made for you, so finish your own to-do list first.

4. Focus on the top 3 important tasks per day

Always ask yourself *"If I completed these things, would it be a good day?"* If those are all you need for a good day, then why not complete those? Because if you have a to-do list with 20 items, you'll never get them all done. And you'll probably concentrate on the easiest tasks anyway. The exact number of tasks can vary. For those of you who follow the Ivy Lee method, the magic number will be six, while Warren Buffett fans may prefer five, but it is definitely on the lower side.

5. Once you know how to do something, write down the steps needed

This might seem a pointless exercise, but remember that you can always miss something, especially once you start having several clients contacting you for jobs. So why not list what to respond, when to respond, how much time to allocate to what, when to start invoicing and when to start sending reminders for invoices? Secondly, once everything is written out, you may spot methods of improvement you couldn't notice previously such as creating email templates for your standard responses. Thirdly, should you ever want to expand and maybe hire an assistant, you could just simply copy and paste part of your list of steps and send it.

6. Seek help whenever possible. You'll probably need it!

I noticed my productivity started to increase significantly once I <u>stopped</u> having faith in myself. What I mean by this is I stopped thinking I had great willpower and innate time management skills and decided to treat myself like an employee. That's when I started downloading apps that block websites where I waste time (I use SelfControl for Mac, which is free, and I use it to block Facebook, Twitter, YouTube, etc. etc.). I also found some coffee shops with no internet and started going there to work when I needed to concentrate on something offline. Basically, I tried to make it as easy as possible for me to work and as hard as possible to waste time. Much like a micro-managing boss would.

∙∙∙

If You're Serious about Time Management[11]

For those who are serious about this, the first book to start with is Getting Things Done, by David Allen. I definitely recommend this as a starter book for anyone interested in time management. It will help you visualize what you are trying to achieve and how to divide it into manageable goals and deal with huge time wasters such as email and other small interruptions.

Although the book teaches you to be much more effective and efficient with your time, it does

---

[11] *Disclaimer: At the risk of sounding like a broken record, I am neither getting paid nor receiving any other type of benefit from anyone for naming these books. I just found them very useful.*

have a shortfall you should be aware of and that's how you end up making use of the free time you've left available. If something that used to take you two days now takes you half a day, you will be tempted to spend the other half of the day trying to cram in more. After all, you've been so productive and it feels so good, so why not squeeze in just that bit more?

So, a good additional read on top of my first recommendation is <u>The Four Hour Workweek</u>, by Tim Ferriss. This book is not only full of great tips and tricks, but also explains why you only want to complete those few important tasks rather than cram in more. And instead go for a run or do some other activity. Once again, although it's a great book, I find it also has some shortcomings. For example, you can't really make a plausible 80/20 analysis (a concept I explain later on in this book) before you know where your business is coming from. You need to actually start doing business and recognize the patterns.

Along these lines, the next book I recommend is <u>Work the System</u>, by Sam Carpenter. The idea behind this is great, in that every business needs a system. In fact, every ongoing project and task needs a system. An ideal system is one that the worst worker you know could follow flawlessly. The steps should be very simple and easy to follow.

And this leads to my fourth recommendation: The Checklist Manifesto, by Atul Gawande. This simplifies the process even further and shows how all these great businesses have been managed via the simple checklist. Why doesn't the same type of airplane crash ever happen twice? Because Airlines are great at learning from their mistakes and creating simple checklists for pilots to follow in any type of emergency. You'll see the same process being followed in hospitals where lives are being saved, as well as in many smart businesses. If these important organizations are relying on checklists, your business ought to as well.

As I mentioned, none of these books will give you all the answers in their entirety. But they all have really great points which you can then adapt depending on your needs.

Shares, Commissions, and Rush Jobs

When dealing with clients offering payments in shares or commission, or clients with rush jobs, the basic gist is this: Avoid them! Here's a little more detail on this subject:

Shares and Commissions

You will see this mostly with book translations, where some authors simply can't afford to pay you any rate for their 200,000-word book to be translated and instead offer you a commission based on sales in your language. You may be forgiven for thinking this could be a decent offer, and it might well be, but there are several points against it. **First of all, you are a translator.** You're neither an expert in book sales nor or a literary agent in the book's target market. It may have been a best seller back in Bulgaria, but that doesn't mean it will do well in the United States. In fact, you don't even know if it will be published. And while the author might be getting a translation for free, this also means that they don't have too much skin in the game yet.

190

In other words, you simply don't know what will happen. The world you know is translation, so you can explain that you will get paid as a translator. Secondly, even if the book is successful, there will be a huge delay in payment from the point of translation to eventual publishing and subsequent sales. Therefore, don't be surprised if you have to wait two years to see any kind of payment at all. Third, the author now convinced you to hold a stake in the book's sales, so they'll be probably expecting you to do some, if not all, of the marketing in your target language. After all, you speak the language and the author doesn't. So all of a sudden, you've become a marketer as well. Hopefully that was enough to dissuade you.

One more side note on this subject. Be aware also of being approached by startups. I've been approached in the past by app developers, and they might want to offer shares in their business for translations. If this happens, then go back to the previous paragraph.

Rush Jobs

Go to any job posting website and you will see some postings with *"Rush Job"*, *"Urgent"*, or *"Very Urgent"*. Although this isn't the case 100% of the time, you should be aware that very often <u>these will be problem jobs</u>. Customers who need 5,000 words translated by tomorrow morning are the same who will then find mistakes with your translation or say that the end client complained. They'll ask you for a discount or be very late with their payments. I generally find that the clients with the most relaxed schedules are the most pleasurable to work with and those who also pay me the quickest.

If there is any logic behind this theory, it could be this: any urgent job most likely means that <u>someone along the chain of command is disorganized</u>. After all, that PowerPoint presentation you are translating wasn't just thought up yesterday, and the client meeting it is needed for tomorrow morning wasn't just planned today. And if they were, then someone along the chain of command should have had the wherewithal to notice this might be a bad idea. I'm not saying this is always the case, but it often is. I can often sense the client being pressured by their client or boss, and pass that pressure on to me. In fact, once I even asked the client to tell his boss that giving the presentation in a week's time, rather than the next day, would be more beneficial to everyone, and it worked!

Use Boomerang

This has been a really useful tool for me for collecting payments. Boomerang works with Gmail and probably other email hosts as well. Here's how it works: when you're writing an email, there is a Boomerang option at the bottom of the window that allows you to re-send the same email if, for example, you receive no response within two days, or one week or something. You can also just choose to send the same email multiple times or at various intervals. So, in case you want to chase someone who owes you money and find it hard to remember to email them regularly, Boomerang is a great tool that does this for you.

Your Support System

Do any of the following phrases sound familiar?

1. *"Hey, can you run some errand for me this afternoon, since you're not stuck in the office like me?"*
2. *"Of course you can have another beer! It's not like you have to wake up early tomorrow morning!"*
3. *"So, what do you do all day?"*
4. *"Life's easy for you, since you don't have to deal with a job!"*

Do these phrases irritate you so much you just want to break stuff?

Welcome to the world of being your own boss. Nobody else is going to take you seriously, at least not at first. And why should they? To them, a job is being told what to do, having a boss breath down their neck, following orders and waiting for their paycheck. It is basically a very passive way to live, while yours is the most active imaginable.

Sure, you could sit at home watching TV all day, but then you won't make rent. You have to be your own boss, employee, middle manager and intern all at the same time. And you're still not guaranteed any sort of paycheck. The best analogy I heard is that an entrepreneur is someone who works 16 hour days so they don't have to have a job. So, given all this, it is important to have a support system. This is your livelihood. It's only as real as you make it, so surround yourself with people who understand your world. People who don't understand it can be toxic.

Let's face it, if your friend wants you to pass by IKEA to pick something up because they're stuck in the office, you might be able to oblige them. But realize that by doing so, you're also admitting several things:

1. Your friend's time is more important than your own.
2. You are available in the future for further errands, as long as you don't have a predetermined emergency, and as long as your friend buys you a drink or whatever after it's done.
3. If you can run your friend's errands during work hours, you can also do other stuff rather than work.
4. Your friend's view of your lifestyle is reinforced.

Of course, the best way to avoid this is to surround yourself with other entrepreneurs, freelancers, and people who work for themselves. They will understand that you need your work time

196

and in fact will often help you find the best time and method for getting work done.

Another way is to actually seek out a workplace such as a small office or co-working space. This makes it easier for you to say, "*I'm at work, sorry*". It also has the added benefit of surrounding yourself with other like-minded entrepreneurs.

The main point here is to take your work seriously. It's only as serious as you make it, so be strict about it. If this means telling your friend "*No, I'm at work right now, sorry*", then so be it. Note how they would have given you that answer, and chances are you would give it if you were in a co-working space or your own office anyway. So, when you are working from home, your home is your office. Treat is as such. If your friend complains, then explain that this is your livelihood and you need to take it seriously. A good friend will understand and will most likely respect and admire your self-discipline.

CAT Tools

Since launching my book, I've had a couple people ask me about Computer Assisted Translation (CAT) tools. Those of you who have been translating for some time have no doubt come across them. Clients or fellow translators may ask if you use tools such as Trados or Wordfast. So, what are these and are they really worth it?

What are CAT Tools?

CAT tools are programs that help with the translation process, usually by memorizing certain terms and translations as you come across them for easy reference in the future. You can find a decent

list of CAT Tools here:
http://en.wikipedia.org/wiki/Computer-assisted_translation#Some_notable_CAT_tools.

Do not confuse CAT tools with Machine Translation (MT), which is a translation performed by a machine. CAT tools perform none of the translation for you, but retain the translations you've performed, and usually recreate the format of the original document.

Are They Any Good?

In theory, CAT tools are great and combine both human and machine skills. Machine translation alone can to this day still produce pretty bad translations, but humans also make mistakes, forget past translations, or just get worn out after a while. So, by combining the strength of each, you can achieve optimal results. And, anyone who has been going through a long translation knows how great it is to have the translation for some obscure term pop up automatically, or knows how annoying it is to comb back through old documents in order to find how you translated a certain term.

What's Wrong with Them?

Namely, the cost. The most popular CAT Tool by far is SDL Trados. As of this writing, the SDL Trados Studio 2019 Professional (Single-user) costs **USD**

2,895 (Yes, seriously)[12]. Of course, as a freelancer you can get the simpler *"freelance"* version which starts at **USD 845** and goes up from there. The next most popular is probably MemoQ, which costs **EUR 620 or USD 770**. And another popular one is Wordfast, which costs **EUR 400**.

By the way, if you have a Mac, you won't be able to use Trados, MemoQ or a host of many other tools. In theory they say they *"can be"* compatible with Mac, but I wouldn't count on it.

Now, some will argue that the time you save by using a CAT tools helps you recoup the money spent on it, but I disagree. Bear in mind that the memorized terms generally must be entered by the user. There is no internalized dictionary or glossary, but it is purely based on your input. So, it might be easier to just develop your own glossary of translated terms (see the glossary section), which can easily be kept in Excel format (or anything else) and can be referred to as needed, or simply kept open.

Another point to remember is that clients often ask for discounts based on repetitions when using CAT tools. Basically, if a certain text has 1800

---

[12] Prices taken from here: https://www.sdl.com/store/

words, they may only pay you for 1500 words because 300 are repetitions. This can make sense at first, but, then again, you paid for the CAT tool in the first place, so even the advantage of having repetitions has a cost. Secondly, this would not work in most other industries. **If a web designer uses similar templates for different website designs, the client doesn't get to pay the designer less. Likewise, a lawyer doesn't get paid less for using similar contracts for different clients.**

Having said that, there are certain occasions in which a CAT tool may be useful. First of all, if you can get a group of translators together to split the cost, then why not? Make sure ahead of time that you can all have access to it, especially if you're all using different computers. If so, can you all use it under the same license? Also, if you have a client who you know with 100% certainty is a repeat client, requires the CAT Tool, and will pay you back the cost of said tool in several months at most, then it can be worth it.

My Recommendation

In conclusion I would not recommend using these tools until further down the line. For now, you can try testing the concept out with some free versions. Admittedly they're not as good, but they can still help you out. One such freebie is *OmegaT* which produces .tmx files. It seems to be the only one actually geared toward individual users rather than agencies. Another one is *Wordfast* Anywhere, which is a web-based, stripped down version of *Wordfast*. You can also try *Across*. This is only for MS Office users, but is it probably the oldest free CAT tool out there.

Glossary

Keep a glossary of the terms, expressions and acronyms you come across. Technically, every time you have to look something up, you should be able to insert it into the glossary so that it can save you time in the future. I keep my glossary on Excel so I can sort it alphabetically and it is easy to search.

Excel allows you to sort something alphabetically after the fact, and by whichever column you choose. To do so, highlight all columns in use and include all the cells to be included, then click on Data→Sort. If you want to sort everything alphabetically by Column A, then choose Column A, Ascending.

Translation Tips

As was mentioned in the introduction of this book, here you will find tips for everything other than translation itself. This is due to the fact that translation tips per se are much easier to come by than tips for setting up your translation business and earning a living off of it.

There is also the fact that it is almost impossible to give translation tips that will be useful to all of you. There are over 7,000 languages out there right now. But, even if we only count the top 23 languages, remember that this would entail 23x22 (that's 506) different[13] language combinations, further subdivided by every specialization out there[14]. As you can imagine, it is hard to generalize with all of those different requirements.

However, I would be remiss if I didn't include at least a few general guidelines to keep in mind:

---

[13] That's 23 languages combined with one other language, obviously not counting the same language combined with itself.

[14] Remember, if you do require more customized help, you can always contact me for a 1-on-1 session here: **http://tiny.cc/Coaching**

- First of all, when translating between two languages, it's generally assumed that you are either fluent in both, you have lived in both countries, or you've formally studied one of the languages. As mentioned before, your native tongue should be the target language.

- You will notice that some terms, like job titles, can be interchangeable, such as *"secretary"* and *"administrative assistant"*, or *"CEO"* and *"President"*. So feel free to ask your clients for past translations or documents, so that you can get their terminology correct. If they have been translating expressions in a certain way thus far, you might as well find out about it right away rather than be corrected after having translated the document.

- Always remember that acronyms can be different across languages, e.g. *"U.N"*. vs. *"N.U."*, or *"E.U."* vs. *"U.E."* It is better to check them all the first time you come across them, and then include them in your personal glossary (mentioned above).

- Become familiar with *"Track changes"* on Microsoft Word (found under "Tools"). This is especially useful for editing, proofreading, and comparing translations. Be comfortable with leaving comments as well ("Insert"→"New Comment" in Microsoft Word).

- Keep bookmarks of useful sites and sites you find yourself using for any translation. Chances are you will want easy access to these at some point in the future. You can find some useful links in our Resources section as well.

Computer Backup

In short, you should always have one. A translator's entire career depends on his or her computer, so use some form of backup such as an online tool like Dropbox, Google Cloud or an external hard drive, an extra computer, or an automatic backup program like Backblaze, iCloud or Carbonite.

The important thing is to remember to back your files up regularly. Ideally once per day. This is why I recommend an automatic backup system, so everything gets backed up automatically without your having to worry about it. The important thing, however, it to back everything up. Redundancy isn't bad, either. As an example, I use Backblaze for automatic backups, I use Dropbox regularly for big files even when I am still working on them, and I periodically back everything up on an external hard drive just for good measure.

Computer Software and Hardware

This may or may not seem obvious, but regardless, there are certain programs that you should probably have no matter what. One essential tool is MS Office. You will have clients sending you documents in MS Word, PowerPoint, and the like. While there are free versions of these that claim to be compatible with the originals, from what I've seen there are a great number of bugs in these and they can cause a great deal of headache.

You will also need a decent internet connection. Once again, you will be dealing with clients who will expect you to be able to respond quickly and download any of their files in a timely manner. A stable and reliable internet connection for getting work done, doing your research, searching for terms is indispensable and you simply can't rely on your phone while using data. Get a decent internet connection that you can rely on.

Another one is Skype. Yes, there are more advanced and cooler programs out there for video calling, but they all come with a learning curve and most of your prospective clients will be used to Skype and will want to use that. You'll also need a decent microphone and webcam, if one isn't built in already. Once again, you might not need these for the translations per se, but speaking with your clients face to face can be very useful when establishing trust.

A Word about Translators vs. Editors

As a translator, you may have to work with editors, you may get hired as editor, and then you may have to work with translators. For this reason, there are a couple things to keep in mind, since translators can often find themselves working against editors, and certain clients like to use this to their advantage. This is rare but it's good to keep in mind nonetheless.

Briefly, a translator is hired to translate the text from one language to another. Then, an editor is often hired to check the translator's work and make sure it is accurate.

Problems can arise here because, in a sense, the editor is paid to find mistakes with the original translation. So even if the translation has been carried out correctly, editors may try to find mistakes just to show that they are earning their pay.

The problem here is that the client may be surprised by the number of mistakes, and then refuse to pay the translator or seek a discount. The translator may then try to find mistakes with the editor's edit work until, sooner or later, the editor and the translator are working against each other. The result? Both the editor and the translator will earn less money after a lot of haggling back and forth, and the only winner will be the client.

So How Do You Avoid This?

Luckily, there are some ways to minimize the chances of this happening. The first, as always, is to make sure you do a good job. It is much harder to find mistakes with a job well done.

The second method is to put yourself in the other person's shoes. If you are an editor and you come across a translation that is done well, realize that you don't necessarily have to cover it in red to show that you are doing your job. You can also just provide a thorough analysis after the fact by saying something like "this translation was done very well. I especially liked the translator's use of technical terminology in Section Two, which is proper considering the target market of this report". You might also see a translation that is acceptable, even though you would rather use a different expression. This doesn't necessarily denote a mistake, but just a difference in preference. In this case you, as an editor, can say something like *"Section Two was correct, but I felt that the terms were a bit too technical given the target market, so I changed the expressions around to suit this"*.

Now if you, as an editor, find egregious mistakes, then you should feel free to call the translator out on them, since that is precisely what you were hired to do.

If on the other hand, you are on the other end of this equation and working as a translator, there are things you can do too. When you receive corrections by an editor, in order to avoid a back and forth of nasty comments, you can say something like *"the editor's changes are correct, but I still prefer my wording for this section, given that most of the target audience will be familiar with these technical terms"*. This confirms that the editor's version is correct, as is yours, which should make both of you look better than any back and forth infighting.

What About Back Translations?

The same can often happen with translators performing something called *"back translations"*. Briefly, back translations are translations from the target language back into the source language. These are used as a method to check the original translation, and are often used mostly in the legal and medical fields, although they can be occasionally found in any field.

So basically:

LANGUAGE A---------*Translation* →LANGUAGE B -----
Back Translation →LANGUAGE A

What may happen here is that the result of the back translation shows some big differences when compared to the original text. In this case, the client may try to blame either the first translator or the second. Usually it's both. Here again, it is up to the translators to put themselves in each other's shoes. If two different expressions are interchangeable, then the differences might be acceptable.

Of course, as always, if there are egregious mistakes then you should feel no guilt in calling them out.

Setting Your Own Schedule

No one said you have to work from nine to six. You can decide what works best for you, although ultimately it will also depend on your clients. For example, I am currently based out of the United States, while most of my clients are in Europe. This means I am usually up quite early dealing with work, but I'll be finished by early afternoon. On the other hand, while I am in Asia, I can sleep in, but I'll usually work until pretty late, even though I might be drinking a beer while I work! But also experiment a bit. Can you get a lot of work done on weekends? Great! Chances are you can use that by completing jobs over the weekend, which many other translators cannot do!

Passing the "So What?" Test

I read about this in an excellent sales book called *"New Sales. Simplified"* by Mike Weinberg. It not my original thought, but I really like this particular idea he talks about in his book called the *"So What"* test, which works like this:

When you are writing your introductory letter or your email to clients, are you writing things like:

- *"I can translate 4,000 words a day."*
- *"I have been a translator for 20 years."*
- *"I grew up bilingual."*
- *"I use CAT tools."*
- *"I don't use CAT tools."*

Great. Now try adding *"So What?"* as a response to each one:

- *"I can translate 4,000 words a day."* **So what?**
- *"I have been a translator for 20 years."* **So what?**
- *"I grew up bilingual."* **So what?**
- *"I use CAT tools."* **So what?**
- *"I don't use CAT tools."* **So what?**

The problem with these phrases is that they are all about your skills and what you do. But you can turn your 'skill' into a 'benefit' for the client with something like:

- *"I can make your website stand out in a crowded market."*
- *"I can help your correspondence flow smoothly between your New York and Hong Kong offices."*
- *"Do you want a competitive advantage when dealing with Spanish speaking customers?"*

Or even something like:

- *"Do you want a friendly and efficient translator to do business with?"*

Ideally, you can find your own strong points, and describe how they benefit the clients, so they don't have to. Remember that most end clients have no idea what CAT tools are or how many words they need translated per day. Regardless, when you're writing to them, make sure to keep in mind how this can BENEFIT THEM, not just how skilled you are and what you're capable of.

My Language Combination Is Too Rare / Too Common

I've heard both of these complaints. Some translators will complain that there isn't enough demand for their rare language combination, so how are they supposed to earn a living? Other translators, on the other hand, will complain that their language combination is too common and there are already too many translators doing what they do.

In fact, I will guess that one of these two issues has worried you since you started out, correct? Well, the fact is you don't need to worry about this issue for either option.

Let's start with the language combinations that are rare. I've worked with a translator who specializes in Karen-English translations. Have you heard of Karen? Probably not. Well, it is a language spoken in parts of Eastern Myanmar and Western Thailand. As you might imagine, there isn't much demand for this language. On the other hand, there aren't many translators in this language combination, so when translations involving Karen need to be carried out, this one translator will almost always be contacted.

216

At the opposite end of the spectrum, there is an oversupply of translators. I recently attended a meeting of Carolina Association of Translators and Interpreters (CATI), and out of around 30 attendees, there were only two of us who didn't translate to or from Spanish. So, Spanish-English translators who are just starting out might feel extremely discouraged to see all this competition. But the fact is that the local court and government system is constantly searching for more Spanish translators, and there is a constant shortage.

Basically, if you have a rare language combination, there might be a low level of demand, but there will also be a low level of supply. Equally, if you have a more common language combination, there will be a lot of supply, but also a lot of demand to match.

These two situations are probably quite different. Spanish translators will probably have to market themselves more when first starting out, but both cases present opportunities, so don't despair!

Certification

There are several versions of this that you may encounter, and to tell the truth, it can mean different things in different countries. I have often found that even clients often aren't sure what they require, so it might be beneficial to cover some of the basics here.

Certified Translator

First of all, if someone wants a **certified translator**, this usually means they want the translator to have an official translation certification from, say, the ATA (American Translator's Association) or equivalent in another country. Many schools also offer translation certification, which you can usually attain by passing a translation test in your language combination. Of course, many of these tests can be quite expensive and very difficult, so do your research before actually taking one.

My recommendation is not to let this delay starting out, which is why I only mention it here and not in the beginning. In other words, start out translating and, while you are doing so, you can look into taking a test that provides you with official certification somewhere. It will be an investment of time, money and effort, and you can certainly be earning money in the meantime. And after a while maybe you will have a better idea as to whether you want to obtain certification or not.

Certified Translation

The second thing you might see is that someone wants a **certified translation**. This is actually a completely different thing. It usually means they want the translation certified (and/or notarized) by a lawyer (and/or notary public). Here this can vary a lot from country to country (and even region to region within a country). For example, in Switzerland a certification requires a visit to the lawyer's office and will cost the equivalent of several hundred dollars at least. In the United States, however, you can often find a notary public at your local UPS store who can handle the entire job for around $10. So check to make sure you know what type of certification, notarization, or apostille the client requires before proceeding.

Terms of Service - 5 Things You Can Add

This was touched upon previously in the book. When stating your terms of service, there are several things you can include if you don't feel too awkward doing so. I find that the best time to include this information is in the email that confirms you're accepting the job, so that the client can see it and hopefully accept all terms before you actually get started.

I've provided an outline below for you to tweak and fill in the blanks. Of course, these are merely meant as examples to show some of the options you have:

1. *"The translated text will be deemed accepted and satisfactory if no inquiries have been made within 7 days of delivery."*
2. *I retain full ownership of the translated text until full payment is received.*
3. *This contract is between (YOUR NAME) and (AGENCY NAME), without reference to any end client or third party.*
4. *An opportunity will be given to the translator for corrections, deliverable within 48 hours from notification.*

5. *My minimum charge is: XXX. I charge YYY extra for DTP services, urgent work, and technical translations."*

SOME OTHER STEPS TO TAKE IF YOU WANT TO SEE HOW MUCH YOU CAN GROW

Next Steps

Keep in mind that nothing in this particular chapter and the one following it is obligatory. If it's too much work for you, or you can't be bothered, and you're happy doing what you're doing, then by all means, skip these chapters. These next steps are purely for those who want to keep pushing and see how much they can actually get out of this. Also, you shouldn't start the steps in these two chapters until you have a good client base and you find yourself with too much work on your hands.

However, if you find yourself inundated with requests that you can't take care of, if you want to earn money, but don't want to work 18 hours a day, and if you would like to push your limits and see what you can accomplish, then by all means, keep reading.

Your steps, roughly speaking, will be divided into **delegating** and **managing**. Also, realize that, at the beginning, this will entail more work, not less. But, if you do it right, it could pay enormous dividends over the long term.

Incorporation

Your absolute first step should be to incorporate your company. In fact, you should probably complete some form of incorporation regardless, since it is likely advantageous to you for both tax purposes and legal purposes. This is far beyond my purview, since laws vary depending on state and country and they change all the time. I was incorporated in Oregon and I was able to complete everything online for a nominal fee of $60 USD. I then went to Bank of America to open a corporate account, and they even called the IRS to obtain a Tax Identification Number (TIN) for me at no extra charge (although their helpfulness may have had more to do with the fact that I was in Portland than that it was Bank of America).

I recommend completing this step right away because it is relatively easy and inexpensive. It cost me less and it took me less time than signing up for some of these translator websites, and it can be great for various reasons, whether you decide to become an agency or not.

First of all, **it shows you're serious** for potential clients. Again, you won't sound like a "freelancer", who might not be around in a month, but you sound like a real business. Secondly, it allows you to **work with businesses on a more equal footing**. This will help them take you more seriously for payments and terms. Thirdly, you'll be able to receive **tax benefits**. This will vary depending on your country, region, state, canton or province, but chances are that company incorporation has a more beneficial tax structure than a person does. Fourth, this can be **a lifesaver for liability**. You never know whom you will encounter over the internet, so if a client decides that you ruined their business and wants to sue you, they could theoretically go after everything you own and all your personal savings, unless you're incorporated. If you are incorporated, however, you never need to worry about being personally liable.

As you could probably tell from my invoice, I incorporated under the name Acahi (now Lugano Translations), which has now become the name of my company. Even when I perform the translations myself, I invoice the clients using that form. No client has had any issue with it thus far, and should some big problem occur in terms of liability, I know I am covered.

I will not go into the types of incorporation here, since they differ for each country. This book being in English, however, I will give you some links here for incorporating in the UK, US, Canada and Australia:

UK: http://en.wikipedia.org/wiki/Company_formation

US: http://www.bizfilings.com/learn/compare-company-types.aspx

Canada: http://www.canadabusiness.ca/eng/page/2853/

Australia: http://asic.gov.au/for-business/starting-a-company/how-to-start-a-company/

Naming Your New Company

How much time should you spend deciding on your new company name? Well, as an example, I chose the name *Lugano Translations* because I started my business in Lugano and I deal with translations. Pretty simple, right?

As you can tell, I don't believe any time should be wasted in choosing a snazzy company name. Remember, the name *Google* was a typo (it was supposed to be googol). Adidas was a contraction of the founder's first and last names (Adolf Dassler). Adobe was named after a creek behind the founder's house. And I doubt any focus group would have chosen Microsoft or Virgin as strong-sounding company names.

Having said that, I do recognize that I may be somewhat extreme in my nonchalance here. So, if you do want to research a good name, I would just give several suggestions:

1. The dot.com should be available **without dashes or other odd symbols**.
2. You should be able to convey the name over the phone **without having to repeat it** multiple times.

228

3. Try not to make the name **too long or have it contain too many** syllables.
4. Make sure it's **not already taken.** The dot.com and incorporation process should pretty much take care of this, but check the site below if you're still uncertain (and you're in the United States).
http://tmsearch.uspto.gov/
5. Adding *"translations"* to the end of the name, both on the website and elsewhere, is also usually a good idea.

Of course, I'm not really sure Lugano Translations fulfills the second and third of these points, but it is easy to spell if need be. The main mistake people make with a company name tends to be over-investment. No matter how much significance it has for you, essentially it is a form of marketing, since its main purpose will be conveying your image. If you want to spend a lot of time with your image, I think a logo would be more worth your while than the company name. For the record, I had my logo done on fiverr.com for $20 USD. Another good source is 99designs.

80/20 Analysis

What if you're not sure? You have plenty of work, but could you be doing better? Should you tell a pain-in-the-neck client to buzz off? Well, this is your business now. One of the great things about this is that you get to choose what you want to do and with whom you want to do it. As a general rule, I find that a periodic 80/20 analysis of my clients and my work helps me out tremendously.

The 80/20 analysis, otherwise known as the Pareto Principle, is a very useful principle for your translation practice. Wikipedia, states that *"for many events, roughly 80% of the effects come from 20% of the causes."* So how does this apply to what you do?

Well, many people in many different walks of life have started using this as a general rule of thumb. More specifically, for your business, you may find that:

- 80% of your profits come from 20% of your customers.
- 80% of your complaints come from 20% of your customers.

- 80% of your profits come from 20% of the time you spend.

The ratio need not be strictly 80/20, but more often than not it will be even more dramatic than that[15] and an analysis of this sort can often lead to great gains. For example, if 80% of profits come from 20% of the time you spend, and you are spending 80% of the rest of the time for just 20% of the profit, it makes sense to drop what you do 80% of the time, even if you risk losing 20% of your profit. This is because if you redirect these efforts to what is earning you 80% of your profits, chances are you will end up earning much more with less effort.

As a hypothetical example, let's say you have client A who is as smooth as silk to work with. She assigns a translation with a deadline, you accept and deliver on time, and then you get paid promptly. Now, let's say you have client B, who assigns a translation, then changes the deadline, has a tendency to require further changes once you've delivered, wants to chat with you too often via Skype, and often delays payment.

---

[15] The book "The 1 page Marketing Plan" states you should apply 80/20 to 80/20 itself, which produces a 64/4 rule, or basically 96% and 4%

What should you do? Obviously, client A is the better choice, but client B may be paying you decently as well. However, after an 80/20 analysis, you realize that all the time spent on client B pays much less per hour spent than client A. At this point and so you have several options:

1. You could decide to cut out client B completely and concentrate more on clients that resemble client A, using your newfound spare time to find other similar clients. Or you can simply use that spare time in other ways, since you're still earning 80% of your profits.

2. Alternatively, you could contact client B and lay down certain ground rules, such as new payment terms or a maximum number of change requests or Skype conversations for example. You don't have to be mean about it, but you can be firm, and specify that your other clients follow those protocols. The worst-case scenario here is that they don't do business with you anymore, which might be a good thing anyway.

So, regardless, periodic 80/20 analyses are great. In fact, you should probably be applying them to most activities you perform.

Delegating

The first step here is to **find a good translator**. In other words, you want to find someone like you were when you first started following the steps outlined in this book. Clearly, you want someone who knows what they're doing, but are just starting out. How do you find this person? On the same websites where you started out. I would suggest Upwork.com. Here you might have to dig a little deeper, but you will find people who are just starting out and haven't been able to pay the fees for better sites yet. If you do your homework well, chances are that you will find someone worth their weight in gold.

Remember not to feel guilty about paying this translator less than what you are receiving. In his or her eyes, you have several things he or she doesn't.

- Experience
- A client (probably more than one steady client)
- Project management skills
- Your reputation, which is at stake with the end client

Your first couple of jobs will be to test this translator. This means you will have to go over the translation yourself to check everything. If there

234

are certain issues, feel free to mention them to the translator. Back and forth communication is essential to a long-term relationship, and most translators who are worth their stuff are open to suggestions.

This will also mean more work on your side, as well as more time needed, so make sure the deadline you give is earlier than the client's deadline. You never know if this translator will deliver on time, will completely mess something up, or even just disappear. Be ready for anything.

Once you have found a good translator, the next step is to **find a good editor**. This editor should resemble the translator, but possibly be more eloquent and grammatically precise, if possible. It is theoretically possible to find a good editor while finding a good translator, but trying to test out two new people at the same time can be quite a bit of work so I would suggest concentrating on one at a time.

Do I Need An Editor?

There is an argument for not hiring an editor. After all, if you went through so much effort to find a translator you like and whom you can trust, why bother diluting your earnings even more by finding an editor?

I would counter that, if you feel comfortable being the editor yourself, then by all means, skip this step. If, however, you want to work on other things entirely, you should at least have a good editor available for when you don't have the time. This way you have a system that allows you to step back entirely. The beauty of this is that you might be on vacation in Tahiti, receive a client request, and still be able to delegate it effectively without having to worry about it.

In other words, a good editor gives you peace of mind. There is no rule that you have to use the editor for each and every job, but having one is still a good idea.

The best way to test the editor is to give him or her the translation performed by the translator you trust. Remember, the editor is paid to find mistakes and possible improvements, so this is also a good way of keeping the translator honest.

A couple of pointers:

- **Stick to languages you know.** Chances are the requests you receive are for your working languages. Even if they aren't, stick to languages you know well when delegating. You never know when something might go wrong, and when it does, you'll want to be able to jump in and take care of it right away.

- **Get more than one of each**, if at all possible. Any translator, no matter how reliable, may go on vacation, get sick, find a client they prefer to you, or be unavailable for many other reasons. It is always best to have more than one translator available, just in case. More than two seems like overkill to me, at least at the beginning, but if you have two translators and two editors you can rely on, you're pretty much golden.

- **Get to know your translators well.** Talk to them, keep them updated on what you're working on, add them on Facebook, etc. You will be relying on them, and you presumably you'll want to keep them for the long-term. This will be much more likely if they also see you as a friend, even an online one, and not just an anonymous job provider.

Project Management

In addition to any translations you may be working on, you'll also be managing the projects. If you can afford it, it might be best to take a break from translating while you're building up your business.

What is project management exactly? Well, it is exactly what it sounds like. You are managing both the client and the freelancer. In other words, you'll be relaying information back and forth, making sure both sides are clear as to what is happening, and making sure both sides are happy with the arrangement at all times. Remember, it is *your* reputation that is at stake with either side, so make sure you are being clear.

Once again, this may differ for each person, but I find that the best way to deal with a translator is to be extremely clear about what is expected in terms of the type of translation, deadline, any format requests and so on. You may feel as if you are treating them like a little kid at times, but I find that they appreciate the clarity. Don't leave them to their own devices. They want to complete the translation as per your request, and not have to guess what the client might want.

I usually tell the translator everything I expect and then ask them if and how they will complete it. This forces them to reiterate what I asked them, so I can make sure it's clear.

I also like to be in touch with them over Skype or some form of instant messenger. This just makes them more accessible and also allows me to see if they are online and hopefully working.

Remember, **any issue you have with your translator or editor that is not language-related is probably your fault.** Managing isn't necessarily hard, but it is necessary. The idea is that one day you will be able to step away without losing sleep. In order to do so, you must make sure you are completely in sync with your freelancers. This *will* take time and effort, especially in the beginning.

Are You Making Money?

You found translators and editors and you have clients giving you jobs. But are you sure all of this work is worth it? If the client is paying you $0.10 USD per source word, and you're paying the translator $0.06 USD, while paying the editor $0.04 USD, then clearly something is wrong.

Even if you're paying the translator and editor $0.08 USD per source word total, is it worth the $0.02 USD per word profit to go through the trouble? Well, not if you're translating a 200-word document. But if you're translating a whole book, then possibly.

Obviously, every person is different. Your first step (in case you haven't figured it out yet) is to make sure you aren't paying more than you are earning. If you are making a profit, then you're fine. Here, my suggestion would be to give it a few months. Jobs can be sporadic and different, but if, in the long term, you find yourself earning more money for less work, then it's working out well. If, however, managing these translators is a constant headache, and your extra profit is low, and it is possibly taking time away from your own translations, then it might not be worth it.

I find a good time frame is three to six months, and I usually try to separate what I'm delegating from what I'm working on myself. For example, if my delegation makes me 50% of the cash I usually make, but only takes up 20% of the time a translation would take, then I could, theoretically, spend 50% of the time I spend translating and make 120% of the cash I did before. Clearly, the amount of time spent has to be estimated.

In other words, conduct an 80/20 analysis (see the chapter on 80/20 analysis above).

What Do I Tell Clients?

Very often this is what most readers are wondering and what is stopping most of you from setting up a business. Is this a real business? Are you just being sly about outsourcing your work? How official is the whole thing?

At this point, you are no longer the translator. Nor are you the editor. But you are still responsible to the client for the work. The more tempting solution is to not say anything to the client, since it just takes extra effort for nothing in return. After all, the final translation is still going to come from you, right?

241

Well, chances are this is true, although you can never be sure. For example, Microsoft word keeps track of the initial author of a document. The end client might, perchance, click on the document information and see someone else's name. This is improbable, but certainly not impossible. So, let's take a look at the points in favor of telling and not telling the client.

In Favor of Not Telling:

- It's unlikely they will find out or that anything will change with the end client.
- If the client knows, they might not like the idea of dealing with a middleman.
- The client might want the freelancer to sign the same documents you did.
- If the client has the freelancer's contact info, nothing stops the client from avoiding you and dealing directly with the freelancer at a cheaper price.

In Favor of Telling:

- The client may find out anyway, which makes you look sneaky.

- The translator might make mistakes you may overlook (and then need to explain to the client).
- You cannot outwardly refer to yourself as an agency if you are technically performing all the translations.
- If you don't tell the client, you will have to watch your wording for all future jobs, such as *"I've been working on this,"* rather than *"we've been working on this."*
- It is the ethical thing to do.
- It's also very likely (depending where you are) the legal thing to do.

In essence, my recommendation is to always be fully transparent with the client. What usually happens is the client doesn't care and they're happy dealing with you, as long as you can guarantee the same quality and same service.

If, however, the client has an issue, you always have the option of performing the translation yourself and delegating another translation you might be working on to the freelancer.

Also, if you are forthcoming and honest, you will find yourself much more at ease. As time goes by, if you've been having to watch what you say for a while, life can get pretty stressful.

Do I Create a Contract with Freelancers?

Here again, different people may have different opinions. A contract can cover all your bases in case the freelancer does something wrong. Also, signing a contract can make the freelancer feel more like they are part of your team. You can find sample fill-in-the-blank contracts all over the internet. Try legalzoom.com in the US or Lawbite.com if you're in Europe, or other similar websites.

On the other hand, I don't see any real reason for this. As long as you have written confirmation from a freelancer such as an email, it tends to carry the same weight as any ready-made contract you might want to use. If you use Upwork or similar websites, you can count on the website itself carrying more legal weight than anything you can come up with.

So, here my personal preference is to make sure I have written confirmation of the freelancer's duties for each job, whether this be via email, a website, or even a text message. Just make sure the translator agrees in writing to the job details like the word count, the deadline, and the fee and you should be fine.

If you feel more at ease or feel you will sleep better at night having some sort of contract, then by all means use it. You can tell the freelancer that it is standard operating procedure. They will sign it once and you can forget about it for a while.

Conclusion

And that's pretty much how I was able to achieve this nomadic, but well-paying lifestyle that I'm hoping you can too. I say *"pretty much"* because I simplified it a great deal. If I had to include every wrong turn and false start that I made, this book would be a confusing collection of half-baked approaches and constant restarts from the beginning. I included some of the mistakes I made and in great detail when necessary as I thought this would help you avoid the same pitfalls.

Another reason is that some other approaches didn't work for me, but they might work for you, so I see no sense in knocking them just because I couldn't make them work. For instance, my initial plan was to specialize in book translations. This was because I've always been fond of books, and as an off-and-on author, I sympathize with authors trying to reach new markets. So I thought I could help upcoming authors get their books translated for new markets.

Well, I ended up translating exactly one book that was a textbook on marketing. The translation was merely so the professor could list himself as being published in several languages, in order to get tenure, or something along those lines. After my disillusionment with that experience and seeing how little it paid per word, I decided to concentrate on other types of translations.

But who's to say translating books doesn't work out great for you? They tend to be longer projects with more guaranteed income and more predictable deadlines. So they might be just the thing you need.

Also, I don't mention online advertisements, such as using Google Adwords or Facebook ads. I actually tried these for a while, but found they were a lot of work as well as being a bit too costly for little or no return. Unfortunately, you are competing for views with other advertisers, many of whom are experts in this type of advertising, so I believe the chances that you will succeed the first time around are very slim. Then again, they might have worked for someone else. If they have worked for you, please do let me know and I will be happy to write about it in future editions of this book.

In short, everyone's experience is unique. If you want to share yours, I'd love to hear about it. I may start listing some of them on our website just so translators can start learning from each other more.

Thanks for reading! Now go create your own success story and build your own life, according to your own standards.

Also, if you found this useful, I would really appreciate a review on Amazon! Reviews are extremely useful in helping others get an idea as to what the book is about and what to expect from it. It also really helps me as an author in getting the book out there. Remember, the reviews don't need to be long or detailed!

Thank you!

Robert Gebhardt

Freelance Translator

Useful Links

To Sign up as a Freelancer:

www.upwork.com

www.freelancer.com

www.workana.com

www.peopleperhour.com

To Sign up as a Freelance Translator:

www.ProZ.com

www.Translatorscafe.com

www.Translatorsbase.com

www.addlance.com

www.Twago.com

www.Machdudas.de

www.Translationdirectory.com

www.Traduguide.com

www.Translatorswork.com

Translation Associations:

- https://www.atanet.org/ (*American Translators Association*)
  - o https://www.atanet.org/chaptersandgroups/chapters.php *(various chapters of the ATA)*
- http://www.najit.org/ (*National Association of Judiciary Interpreters and Translators*)
- http://www.fit-ift.org/ (*International Federation of Translators*)
- https://literarytranslators.org/ (*American Literary Translators Association*)

For Help With Translations:

www.ProZ.com/kudoz

www.wordreference.com

www.linguee.com *(takes millions of examples from the web, and sees how they were translated by others in different contexts)* https://context.reverso.net/ *(operates in the same way as linguee.com)*

https://www.translatorsbase.com/about_glossaries.aspx?t=0

http://translate.google.com *(although anathema for some, Google Translate (or bing translate) can be quite useful for terms or expressions not within your expertise).*

http://translate.bing.com

www.translationdirectory.com/dictionaries.htm

www.systranet.com

http://www.online-translator.com/

http://www.translationdirectory.com/free_translators.htm

For Rating Companies (And Seeing How They Are Rated By Others):

www.ProZ.com/blueboard

www.translatorscafe.com/tcutils/EN/search/agencies.aspx

http://www.translationdirectory.com/non-payers.htm

Translator Forums:

http://www.translationdirectory.com/forum/

http://www.translatorscafe.com/cafe/quicklook.asp?TID=152862

http://www.ProZ.com/forum/

Setting up a Website:

http://about.me

http://wordpress.com

http://www.blogspot.com

http://www.tumblr.com

Social Networking

http://www.Linkedin.com

http://www.facebook.com

http://www.twitter.com

http://www.IFTTT.com *(links blogs to social networks and social networks with each other)*

Books Mentioned:

David Allen – *Getting Things Done* - http://www.amazon.com/Getting-Things-Done-Stress-Free-Productivity/dp/0142000280?tag=acahi-20

Tim Ferriss – *Four Hour Workweek* - http://www.amazon.com/The-4-Hour-Workweek-Anywhere-Expanded/dp/0307465357?tag=acahi-20

Sam Carpenter – *Work the System* - http://www.amazon.com/Work-System-Mechanics-printing-September/dp/160832253X?tag=acahi-20

Atul Gawande – *The Checklist Manifesto* - http://www.amazon.com/The-Checklist-Manifesto-Things-Right/dp/0312430000?tag=acahi-20

Mike Weinberg – *New Sales. Simplified.: The Essential Handbook for Prospecting and New Business*

Development - https://www.amazon.com/New-Sales-Simplified-Prospecting-Development/dp/0814431771?tag=acahi-20

Allan Dib – *The 1-Page Marketing Plan: Get New Customers, Make More Money, And Stand Out From The Crowd* - https://www.amazon.com/1-Page-Marketing-Plan-Customers-Money/dp/1989025013?tag=acahi-20

Other:

http://sethgodin.typepad.com/ *(Seth Godin's blog, for marketing)*

http://www.99designs.com *(for designs)*

http://www.fiverr.com *(for designs)*

Glossary

Agency:	Acts as "middleman" between translator and end client. Takes on the risk of non-payment by client and project manages, in exchange for a percentage fee
ATA:	American Translators Association
Back Translation:	Translation from the target language back into the source language
CAT:	Computer Assisted Translation
Comparison:	(For changes in versions) If a document has been translated twice, a comparison ensures that they say the same thing or contain the same information
Editor:	Someone who corrects a translated text, having access to the source text and usually a speaker of the source language
End Client:	The client originally commissioning a translation. May work directly

	with the translator or may use an agency as a go-between
EOM:	End of Month
FIGS:	French, Italian, German, Spanish
IFTTT:	If This Then That
Interpreter:	A person translating spoken word from one language into spoken word in another language. Can be simultaneous or consecutive
Invoice:	Document sent to the client to request payment for work performed
Language pair:	The source and target languages
Localization:	Changing the translation of a target text to suit the target market
MT:	Machine Translation
MT Post-editing:	Editing a text that has been translated by Machine, usually with access to the source language text

NAJIT: National Association of Judiciary Interpreters and Translators

Proofreader: Someone who corrects a text, not necessarily with access to the source language text

SEO: Search Engine Optimization

Source language: Language from which something is being translated

Source text: Text from the original document

Specialization: Area of expertise of a translator

Target language: Language into which something is being translated

Transcription: Listening to spoken words and putting them in writing

Transcription plus translation:

Listening to spoken words in the source language and then writing them in the target language

Translator: Someone who translate written words in one language into written words in another language

Voiceover: Reading a text out loud

Wordcount: The number of words in a
                  document

Freelance Translation Manifesto[16]

I live in the United States and I have noticed an interesting phenomenon. Picture this: two people will be applying for one job. While their expertise and experience may be pretty much equivalent, one of them may speak English with an accent because he or she comes from another country, while the other speaks with no accent, being from the United States. Usually (with the other skills being equal) the job will go to the person without the accent.

Think about it. The accented person applying for that job will not only bring the same skills as the local hire but will also have a completely different point of view to draw examples from. Speaking a different language gives them access to a different mindset, in addition to the local one. In this case, speaking with an accent should be an advantage, but it is rarely so.

Now, do you remember when Mark Zuckerberg spoke to a crowd at the Tsing-hua x-lab

---

[16] Article first featured here: https://medium.com/@oceanlugano/the-freelance-translation-manifesto-f153866ab00a

Session in Beijing back in 2014? News outlets were stunned because he was speaking *"fluent"* Chinese.

The fact is, while not trying to diminish speaking Chinese in public as a second language, Zuckerberg's Chinese was nowhere near fluent, yet he received nothing but praise. In the meantime, the foreigner applying for the job in the US might have been fluent, but just speaking with an accent.

So why are some people praised for speaking two languages, even if one is very limited, while others are penalized for speaking two languages fluently (just retaining a bit of an accent in the second one)?

The main reason I'm mentioning this is because I've seen it in action and I've been the beneficiary of this double standard. For example, in Taiwan a businessman once asked me if I spoke Chinese, to which I replied *"a little bit"* (yi dian dian) – I spoke literally three words and his comment was that my Chinese was so good and he started introducing me to others as someone who spoke Chinese. I doubt this would ever happen with someone traveling or immigrating to an English speaking country saying three words in English.

So what point am I making? Basically what I'm getting at is that there is a dichotomy, with one side taking advantage of the fact that they speak another language, while half, or a majority, of bilingual people feeling almost like their extra language is a disadvantage that they should be able to shed, rather than an advantage to be used to maximum effect.

If you speak more than one language, that is the equivalent of having an extra degree, despite what people might think or say. The main issue is **being able to use that knowledge**. That's where freelance translation comes in.

As I've mentioned before, the translation industry is growing and growing[17]. So, if you speak more than one language, you are well on your way to joining this industry and taking advantage of this fact. Have you been trying to cover up the fact that you speak another language? Have you been pretending like you are monolingual in English? Well, guess what, you actually have an entire industry at your fingertips: it's the translation industry.

---

[17] Read here to see why Google Translate won't be taking any of our jobs anytime soon: https://medium.com/@oceanlugano/is-freelance-translation-worth-it-951142074373

The <u>freelance</u> translation industry is the epitome of what is possible. In this industry you can set up an account online and get started without ever having to work for a company in a physical location. So even if there are no openings in your area or no big companies offering jobs in your language combination anywhere close by, you can always find opportunities online. And working online you can truly let your skills be in control, rather than any type of prejudice.

The fact is, Mark Zuckerberg would not be able to make it as a Chinese translator (don't worry too much about him, he's doing fine). But maybe you could! Just because he gets praised for his language abilities and you don't, this is definitely not a reason to give up on languages.

Freelance Translators are the people bringing the world together. In this age of so many worldwide issues, isn't it worth it to be part of this movement? While using your language, you can earn a living, as well as share ideas, thoughts and opinions with entire populations that didn't have access to them before.

How to Set up a Translation Agency

You may have noticed that all the points in the "*Next Steps*" section follow a certain progression, expanding what you are doing as a freelance translator gradually, working with other translators, being able to offer more services to your clients, etc. What is the final step in this process? Well, it would be setting up your own agency.

As I mentioned at the beginning of this book, that is what I have been doing. I have set up a company called Lugano Translations, using this method, along with quite a few others. Much like my journey to becoming a freelance translator, my journey to setting up a translation agency has had a lot of false turns and losses mixed in with the wins.

If this is something you are interested in, then check out my course "**How to Set up a Translation Agency: The Complete Guide**" available on Udemy (and a couple of other places).

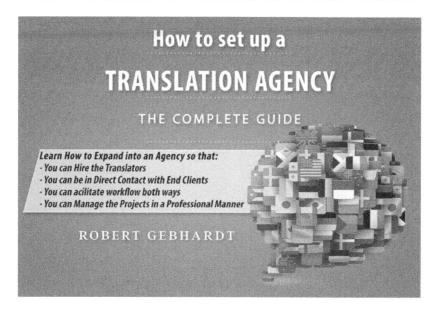

Course Extracts[18]:

This course will help you transition from being a freelance translator to running a full agency. Instead of just relying on one language in order to win business and clients, you can make full use of many languages in order to achieve full potential.

Learn how to expand into an agency so that:

- You can hire translators

---

[18] Available here: http://tiny.cc/TranslationAgencyCourse

- You can be in direct contact with end clients
- You can become familiar with being the go-between and workflow facilitator in both directions
- You can manage projects in a professional manner

Content Overview

This course is structured to serve as reference material, so you can finish the entire course in around one week. However, as your agency grows, you will probably want to go back for refreshers and to see how various steps can apply to your new situation.

Most of this course will be taught via videos, with some written notes and explanations for those wishing to go further in depth.

By the end of this course, you'll be able to use your knowledge to set up and run your own agency. You will understand what exactly you wish to achieve, how to find translators, how to find new clients, and how to maintain the business running with both.

The world is becoming increasingly global, while jobs are less and less secure, and the internet is, by now, near universal. Combine all these factors and you have a perfect storm of opportunity for people who wish to set up their own translation agency!

Don't be limited by the number of hours you can work on a translation or how much you can get paid per hour or per word! Set up a translation agency so you can have other translators work for you!

See what some students have had to say:

"Yes, I am agency owner and it's good to see another colleague's approach." - Matías Hernández

"Thank you so much. The lessons were clear and easy to follow." - Abdi Jiijiile

The purchase of this book entitles you to a discount for the course. Currently this means you pay $19.99 instead of $124.99. So please contact me here: Translation.course@Acahi.com**, and I can mail you the coupon code.**

The way Udemy currently works is that you will have five days in order to redeem the coupon once I send it to you. I wish there were a simpler way to do this, but unfortunately Udemy keeps firm control over its coupons. If a better way comes about, I will update this ebook accordingly. If you are reading this as a physical book, feel free to email me and simply ask.

Do You Need Help with Anything Else?

I also offer other services, namely:

Resume/Profile Page Reviews for Freelance Translators

This includes:

- A review/rewriting (either line by line, or from scratch) of your profile

- Comments and overall thoughts and opinions

- If needed, some tips in case you are planning on using the information for other locations (ProZ.com, LinkedIn, etc.)

- Any follow-up questions or comments you may have.

More information may be required from you as well, such as your CV or other details about your experience.

If This Interests You, Please Follow This Link:
http://tiny.cc/CVReview

Please note: this is a paid service

One on One Consulting

Are you just beginning your journey as a translator? Are you interested in learning the ropes? Or maybe you are stuck at any point along the process and need more customized help related to your specific situation? If so, then a one on one consultation might be ideal for you.

I'm available via Skype, Google Voice, or phone. We can chat about your personal situation and develop a customized approach for you to embark upon this journey of freelance translation. We can also discuss certain aspects you may need help with, such as marketing, sales, setting up, dealing with payments, etc.

If this interests you, please click on this link:
http://tiny.cc/Coaching

Please note: this is a paid service

Regular Consulting Services On A Retainer Basis

I am also available as a regular contact point as you progress through your journey. My services entail:

- A discussion regarding your ultimate goals
- Development of a plan
- Regular consultation to see how your plan is progressing
- Ancillary help for issues and problems that pop up along the way
- Any other help you may require

If this is something that interests you, please email me at Consulting@Acahi.com with a brief explanation of your situation and we can take it from there.

Please note: this is a paid service

Here is what some people have had to say about these consulting and Resume review sessions:

"I would recommend Robert to anybody looking for an efficient coaching session regarding freelance translation or any subject related to it. He can adapt

271

to anybody's specific situation and needs, can answer any question based on many years of experience and will provide you with a clear structure to follow in order to achieve your goals."*- Enrique Llama, English to Spanish translator in Berlin*

"Taking the course "How to be a Successful Freelance Translator" with Robert was really helpful to me. It saved me a lot of time in the learning process on how to start working as a translator. Robert also helped me to design my resume, kindly answered all of my questions and gave me specific additional information via email. I definitely recommend his services."*- Agustín Rodríguez Cuesta – (http://About.me/Agustinrodriguezcuesta)*

"The CV was a tremendous service for two reasons. First, my experiences are quite diverse and he was able to unify them, which took time and listening skills during the consultation. Second, my formatting made him start a new version from scratch, which he did (despite the hassle). The final product was something during my grad experience no one was able to take the time to help me with; he transformed my CV from an educational resume to a Freelance Translators' CV."
- Jadyn Urbina, Spanish to English Translator (http://urbinatranslation.com)

Anything Else?

Am I missing anything? The long and the short of it is that I want to be available for any help you may need regarding freelance translation and your journey to making this your career. No, sorry, let me rephrase that. My real wish is to **make it as simple as possible for you to become a freelance translator**. Seriously. Those of you who watch my YouTube videos might know that I mention it quite often.

Notice how I said I want to make it *"simple"*, not *"easy"*. No matter what, I can't really make it easy, since it isn't going to be a stroll in the park. However, it doesn't have to be too complicated. And while I can't actually do the work for you, I want to be available for you as much as I can while you do the actual work.

So please feel free to contact me at Robert@Luganotranslations.com at any point with any other ways I could help, especially if they don't fall under the points mentioned above.

About the Author

I have been translating ever since I can remember. In high school I started translating documents here and there for extra money, which continued throughout college and grad school. It took me two jobs later to realize that, since translation was always my go-to for extra money, it probably made sense to try making a career out of it. This especially made sense when I realized that most, if not all, my work could be performed over the web, so I could have a web-based job without knowing how to work on websites.

I also work on other projects and I travel a lot, especially between Europe, East Asia and the US. I'm and always happy to meet for a coffee or beer, so feel free to email me and next time I'm in your city we can meet up and talk.

You can reach me at Robert@LuganoTranslations.com.

- Robert Gebhardt

About Lugano Translations

Lugano Translations is the only translation agency offering extra resources for translators. In addition to a YouTube channel (Freelance Translator Tips) with hundreds of videos, our website offers all types of services for people wishing to advance their career in freelance translation, from Resume and Online Profile editing, to one-on-one consulting with individual translators.

You can learn more here: https://luganotranslations.com/translators/

Made in the USA
Monee, IL
27 July 2020